SLICES OF LIFE
STORIES AND DEVOTIONS
FROM A BIBLE TRANSLATOR

ARETTA LOVING

YWAM
PUBLISHING
P.O. BOX 55787 SEATTLE, WA 98155

YWAM Publishing is the publishing ministry of Youth With A Mission. Youth With A Mission (YWAM) is an international missionary organization of Christians from many denominations dedicated to presenting Jesus Christ to this generation. To this end, YWAM has focused its efforts in three main areas: 1) Training and equipping believers for their part in fulfilling the Great Commission (Matthew 28:19). 2) Personal evangelism. 3) Mercy ministry (medical and relief work). For a free catalog of books and materials write or call:

YWAM Publishing
P.O. Box 55787, Seattle, WA 98155
(425) 771-1153 or (800) 922-2143
www.ywampublishing.com

Slices of Life: Stories and Devotions from a Bible Translator
Copyright © 2000 by Aretta Loving

Published by Youth With A Mission Publishing
P.O. Box 55787
Seattle, WA 98155

Loving, Aretta.
    Slices of life from the plate of a Bible translator / Aretta Loving. -- Rev. ed.
        p. cm.
        ISBN: 1-57658-200-0
    1. Loving, Aretta. 2. Missionaries--Papua New Guinea--Biography. 3. Bible--Translating--Biography. 4. Devotional exercises. I. Title.

BV3680.N52L68 2000   266'.009953
                                                                          QBI00-502

To

my ten GRAND kids: Karen and Lyle and Ricky, Michael, and Ryan; Treesa and Mike and Alyssa, Kendra, and Drew. I love you all a zot, zot bit!

the Awa people of the Papua New Guinea (PNG) highlands. My husband and I lived with the Awas off and on from late 1959 into the mid-1970s, and again from January 1994 through October 1997. Some Awas read the translated New Testament and "put truth to [believed in]" Jesus. Of them we say, "We want them in our livers. [We love them.]" Others heard the "Good Talk" again and again, yet rejected it. Thinking of them, we say, "Our livers thirst for them. [We feel deeply for them.]" Many Awas have such great personalities that it is no problem to "want them in our livers"; others—well, they are people just like in any culture!

AMF (American Missionary Fellowship), the mission organization through whom I came to know Jesus Christ.

and my husband, Richard Edward. Honey-Old-Man, as the Awas call him, edits my work and keeps my feet on the ground so I don't write (or do) too many wild things!

Contents

Foreword by Sherwood Eliot Wirt 7

Preface 9

Acknowledgments 11

Prologue "New Guinea"—Our Home! 13

1. Eggs with Eyes 19
2. A God Who Controls the Rain 23
3. Can a Mother Forget Her Child? 31
4. Whirlpools of Worry 35
5. "Don't Do Dat!" 41
6. That Hanging-Upside-Down Feeling 45
7. A Nap Taker's Creed 49
8. Obedience Is Better 53
9. The Old Ones 57
10. Questions, Questions, Questions! 63
11. Furlough or "Whirlough"? 71
12. God's Radio Network 77
13. A Bride for Panuyaba 81
14. The Dark Packet's Power 87
15. Stepping on My Toes 93
16. A Head Lifted High 97
17. TVitis 103
18. The Leaf Has Fallen 107
19. That One-More-Time Bomb 113
20. A Time for Families 119
21. Girl without a Country 123
22. God's Ways Are Not Always Logical 129
23. Jesus Does "Like Light Does" 133
24. Heartbreak 137

25. Would I Mess Up an Opportunity?
    Or Would I Turn a Mess Into an Opportunity? *141*
26. Two Brothers and Two Eggs *147*
27. Cornered and Caught by an Angry Elephant *151*
28. "God Isn't Fair!" *157*
29. Some Things I've Learned from Some
    Very GRAND Kids *163*
30. A Redeemed Symbol *175*

    Epilogue: Like Noisy Children *181*

    Appendix A   *189*
    Appendix B   *190*
    Appendix C   *194*
    Appendix D   *195*
    Appendix E   *198*
    Appendix F   *199*
    Appendix G   *201*
    Appendix H   *204*
    Appendix I   *205*
    Appendix J   *207*

Foreword

Aretta Loving is a choice example of a new species of humanity that has emerged in the twentieth century. I'm not sure what fun names they give themselves, but they are known to people and nations all over the world as Wycliffe Bible Translators.

These folks are unique. They minister, but with their "left hand." They build churches, as it were, with left-handed shovels. They go to the ends of the earth and seek out peoples beyond the ranges, where they witness, pray, heal the sick, care for the young, bring food and clothing, and encourage worship of the true God. But none of these good deeds is primarily why they go.

They have been attacked by Communists, by nationalists, by terrorists, by rebels, by brigands and kidnappers, none of whom understands why they are out there. Their opponents deign to think these people are agents of some greedy international cartel or other.

What is it, then, that the Wycliffe translators do? It is simply that—translate. They aim to make the written Word of God, the Bible, available to every living man, woman, and child on the globe, that people might read, believe, and be saved through the blood of Jesus Christ to the glory of God. That's it! It is the anointed, God-given, right-handed task of Wycliffe Bible Translators. Trained in linguistics and skilled in anthropology, they have made this their work, their calling, and their raison d'être. And this work is made possible through the prayer and support partnership of their family, friends, and churches at home. In *Slices of Life*, Aretta Loving has given us a delightful inside look at this amazing ministry, founded by Cameron Townsend, a student at Occidental College in California in the years of World War I.

Aretta takes us first to the isolated Awa people of Papua New Guinea, where she, pregnant, and her young husband arrive after a two-day trek in the summer of 1959. She settles in to live with the Awa women, children, and pigs and the evil spirits that control the Awa culture. The task: to translate the New Testament into their language.

For the next two hundred pages, we learn how contemporary missionaries live. This is not David Livingstone facing the lions, but a lively American family facing all kinds of issues of health and climate and remote village life and yet determined to get the job done. This kind of work wins awards in eternity.

How does one adapt? How did the Lovings' two lovely daughters survive in such a situation? You will find out. And the situation itself changes as the Lovings find themselves in Kenya, Africa, supervising other translators, who now use computers and other modern tools, and winning the hearts of the local people with hearty demonstrations of love.

At times, the Lovings tour the USA recruiting and training younger Christians to do the same kind of translation work. They use film shot on location and so clarify the ongoing mission for Jesus. What a grand work! And what a splendid insightful book! Aretta Loving has done a signal service to the Kingdom of God and has provided us readers with many hours of inspiration and genuine enjoyment.

SHERWOOD ELIOT WIRT

Editor Emeritus, *Decision* magazine
Former President, Evengelical Press Association

Preface

If you're anything like me, life is a learning process every step of the way. And sometimes your feet may drag. But since "the joy of the LORD is your strength" (Nehemiah 8:10), at times not only will your feet not drag, but they'll jump for joy!

It's taken me over fifty years to discover everything I share here in thirty short chapters (plus a prologue and an epilogue). If you choose, you can cover it all in one month by reading one chapter a day (and squeezing in the prologue at the beginning and the epilogue at the end of the month).

As you read this book, may the spiritual truths wrapped in the stories blanket your heart with warmth. And may you have a clearer assurance of where you fit in God's plan for reaching those who do not know Jesus Christ as Savior and Lord.

Acknowledgments

To those of you who have encouraged me by saying, "You must put your stories in a book!" I say, "Thank you. Each of you has been a Barnabas in my life." And sincere, loving thanks to those of you who've exercised your gift of using a red pen. You've demanded a high standard from me.

Encouragers

Stephen Head is unrivaled in this category. He was director of Member Care in PNG at the time Ed and I were revising the Awa New Testament and I was sneaking in time here and there to give to this book. "How's it going?" he'd often ask.

As a group, Questers from five different sessions encouraged me to "Let us know when you publish a book of your stories."

Susan van Wynen encouraged me immensely. "Most missions books contain great stories only; yours also has 'take-away' value for the reader. And it has potential to reach young people, the group we especially want to see join us in the Bible translation task!"

Editors and Critiquers

My husband first and foremost. From day one, before I sent a story (in perfect shape, of course) to a magazine, he would edit it. Each time, I was sure he had drained his pen of red ink.

Coworkers in PNG—especially Karen Eliason, June Head, Jaki Parlier, Dorothy Price, and Lois Vincent.

And in on the home stretch were WBT editors Susan van Wynen and Martha McNeil. Their excellent suggestions often sparked new ideas for me!

"New Guinea" — Our Home!

To know God's will is life's greatest treasure. To do God's will is life's greatest pleasure.
—Anonymous

TEARS MINGLED WITH PERSPIRATION spilled down my cheeks. "I don't think I can take another step," I sobbed. Yet somehow I pressed on. Up, up, up we climbed, another two thousand feet.

It was August 4, 1959. After I crested that last mountain ridge, I stood looking down into a valley where a couple of dozen small thatch-roofed dwellings nestled.

My legs ached from hours of trekking up and down steep mountain trails. We had hiked through cool rain forest; trudged along expanses of hot, unshaded grassland; picked our way over narrow, rocky precipices; waded through swirling, shaded rivers. It was as we pushed our exhausted bodies up that last 2,000-foot ascent that I cried from fatigue.

But now the sight of that village was enough to dry my tears and cause me to momentarily forget my exhaustion. We had reached Mobuta, the village that was to be our home for much of the next fifteen years!

My husband, Ed, and I, members of the Summer Institute of Linguistics (SIL) and Wycliffe Bible Translators (WBT),[1] had come to the Territory of New Guinea[2] just two months before. At Ukarumpa, our main center, a coworker told us about a group of highland people known by the government as "the Awa." Awa men, he said, were seen around the government patrol post once or twice a year. A band of short, muscular men would emerge from the rain forest, heavily armed with six-foot-long bows and barbed arrows. Twine string, made of bark, braided into their short, fuzzy locks hung down to their waists. Pig tusks stuck through the septa of their noses gave them an especially ferocious look. Since they knew no Pidgin English, the trade language of the territory, no one from "the outside world" could communicate with them. These were the Awa people!

As we heard about these people and prayed for God's leading, both Ed and I received inner confirmation as God's Spirit whispered to our spirits, "These are the people I am sending you to." We would live among the Awas. We would learn their unwritten language, develop an alphabet, and teach them to read. With their help, we would translate the New Testament into their language, and by God's grace, we would see people come to know Jesus.

And now we were stumbling down that last winding stretch of trail that led into the village. We felt tired right down to the bone yet elated to have arrived. The Awa men who had guided us through the mountains[3] proudly and almost regally led us into their village. Men, women, and children silently watched the procession. Our guides put the few essentials we had brought with us in a round, thatch-roofed house about eleven feet in diameter. They then motioned for us to go inside. Feeling too tired to do more, I smiled weakly at the women, then staggered into our new home.

The furnishings consisted of one narrow, low bed built of poles tied together with vines. A mat made from bamboo, which had been flattened and then woven, covered the poles. The house had no windows, and the doorway was barely four feet high. Only after we crawled into our sleeping bags that night did we notice that our bed slanted drastically toward the wall. But never mind the slope, never mind that we'd chosen not to include a mattress as one of those few essentials. We were young; we were blissfully together in our first home as a married couple; and above all, we were thrilled to be living, finally, with the people to whom God had called us.

The author and Isiga standing in front of the Lovings' first home in Awaland.

This was the moment I had looked forward to since I was twelve. The summer before I turned twelve, I had gone to an AMF[4] Bible camp. We slept outdoors under California redwoods at night, heard God's Word proclaimed each morning, and swam in the Russian River each afternoon. There I came to know Jesus as Savior. The next summer, at that same camp, I told God I wanted to be a missionary. My commitment never wavered.

When I was about to enter my freshman year of high school, I argued with my mother, "I don't want to take typing! I'm going to be a missionary, not a secretary." Fortunately, Mom had the final word. Who would have dreamed this missionary would be the secretary who typed drafts of the entire Awa New Testament as many as five times in those years we were translating?

For Ed, our arrival in the village was the fulfillment of a commitment he had made at Virginia Tech. Describing what caused him to make that commitment, he says, "This group claims, 'We have the truth!' That group claims, 'No, we have the truth!' And still another, 'No, we....' So what is truth?' I asked myself."

In his junior year of college, that question had led him to begin reading the New Testament twenty minutes a day. He remembers the day he came across 2 Corinthians 5:17: "Therefore if any man be in Christ, he is a new creature: old things are passed away; behold, all things are become new" (KJV).

"I read those words," he says, "and I just about jumped out of my chair. 'Hey,' I said to myself, 'that's what's happened to me! My life has changed as I've read this book.'"

Later God had challenged Ed with the command to "go into all the world and preach the good news" (Mark 16:15).

Ed felt a quiet inner voice ask, "My son, are you willing to take the good news to people overseas who have never heard it?"

Telling of his reaction to that question, Ed reports, "'Sure, Lord,' I answered flippantly. But the Lord didn't let me read further until I faced up to His question. I got down on my knees and told Him that by His grace, yes, I would serve Him overseas."

Now on this August day in 1959, we had arrived to live among the Awa, a people who had never heard the name of Jesus Christ.

That night, snug and warm under that thatch roof, we slept soundly despite unfamiliar sounds: the grunting of village pigs scratching themselves against the woven bamboo walls, the flapping of huge fruit bats winging through the village, the screeching of a chicken scurrying away from a hungry dog, the friendly chatting that inevitably goes with the stoking of fires throughout the chilly mountain night. Grateful to be there at last, we slept the sleep of the exhausted.

And there we lived for the next four months—just the two of us, until a hen joined us, laying her eggs under our bed!

PRAYER

Father, You are a good Father! I want Your will in my life. I set my will to do Your will so that at the end of my life I can say, "It has indeed been worth it all."

TO MEDITATE ON

[Jesus] said to them, "Go into all the world and preach the good news to all creation." (Mark 16:15)

TO ASK MYSELF

Am I living my life in such a way that should God call me to go to some other country and serve Him, I would hear His voice and obey?

---

1. See Appendix B.
2. In 1959, the Territory of New Guinea was administered by Australia under a mandate from the United Nations. In 1975 it joined with Papua to become an independent nation. The official name of this eastern half of the island is Papua New Guinea, although it is often referred to as merely New Guinea. Papua New Guinea shares this second largest island in the world with Irian Jaya (recently renamed Papua), Indonesia. Approximately 600 surrounding islands of various sizes are also a part of this nation. The waters of the Coral, Solomon, and Bismarck Seas and the Pacific Ocean mark their shorelines.
3. See Appendix C.
4. AMF, American Missionary Fellowship. See Appendix D.

I.

Eggs *with* Eyes

 God is able to do for us exceeding abundantly above what we ask or think, and we are in danger of limiting Him when we confine our desires and prayers to our own thoughts.
—Andrew Murray

AMONG THOSE ESSENTIALS we had brought with us was a small cache of food. *Enough to last six months,* we had thought. Flour, sugar, salt, and yeast—on a one-burner camping stove I would bake bread and eggless cakes in a round bundtlike cooking pan; six cans of peaches in sugary syrup—we'd open one a month; and just over two dozen cans of meat—one for each week.

"We'll eat mostly what the Awas eat," we had agreed. That decision seemed so workable—until after two weeks in the village, when we realized that our first child was on the way! I quickly learned and identified with the Awa word *Anahgonuq*: I am hungry for meat.

During my pregnancy, I also learned about God's unlimited ability to answer prayer. He used—

Eggs with Eyes

"I'm so hungry for eggs," I told the Lord after three weeks in the village. "But...."

I went on to explain to God why I knew it was useless to ask for what I considered impossible. "Lord, there are only a few laying hens in this village, and You know the people keep all their eggs for hatching more chickens. There's just no way for me to get eggs."

I was obsessed with the thought of eggs. I dreamed of them at night; throughout the day I planned the gourmet meal I would prepare with those nonexistent eggs over our outdoor fire.

Finally, in desperation I prayed, "Lord, I can't see *how* You could give me eggs, but please, would You?"

Bright and early the next morning, "Cough! Cough!" alerted us that someone was at the door of our small dwelling. The contrived cough, the Awa equivalent of Knock! Knock!, came from a young man carrying a *lap-lap** with something wrapped in it. As he carefully laid back the folds, he explained the source of the treasure his cloth held. Of his lengthy narration, I understood three words only: Dog eat hen.

That evening as we cooked over our outside open fire, I cracked three of those precious eggs. Plop! plop! plop! into the frying pan they went. Ed stared down at little eyes that peered up at him. He watched me pick out pieces of embryonic eyes, wings, and other nonidentifiable parts. "You can eat all the eggs, sweetheart. Don't feel you need to share any with me," he said.

Scrambled, fertilized eggs! No banquet could have tasted better to my protein-hungry body. But just as we can't live spiritually on past blessings, I couldn't live physically on the memory of the taste of those eggs.

"I can't possibly ask the Lord for more eggs," I reasoned. "Another hen would get killed, and I just couldn't do that to these poor people."

A week later, hunger for eggs once again won over reason. "O God, even if another hen is killed, please send me more eggs."

O me of little faith! It never occurred to me that God could have another way to send eggs, not just once, but week after week for the next three and a half months.

That very afternoon someone came down from the forest with six wild turkey eggs. As I held one of those huge oval balls in my hands, I whispered, "Forgive me, Father God, for trying to figure out how You could answer my prayer instead of just trusting You."

God, my loving Father, owns the cattle on a thousand hills; He owns all the birds of the air, all the chickens on the ground, all the fowls of the forest. And He knew the needs of our Karen while she was still in the womb! He cared that Karen's mother was hungry for eggs. And *He* was not limited by *her* limited imagination.

PRAYER

. Father, thank You that You hear us when we pray. Thank You that You often answer us in creative ways, ways that we could never even imagine!

TO MEDITATE ON

...You do not have, because you do not ask God. (James 4:2b)

God can do anything, you know—far more than you could ever imagine or guess or request in your wildest dreams! (Ephesians 3:20 *The Message*)

The eyes of all look to you, and you give them their food at the proper time. You open your hand and satisfy the desires of every living thing. (Psalm 145:15–16)

TO ASK MYSELF

In what areas of my life do I lack because I fail to ask? Do I limit God because I can't imagine how He could answer some "impossible" prayer?

---

* *Lap-lap* is the Pidgin English word for a long length of cloth worn wrapped sarong-style around the torso, tucked in at the waist. In the 1950s and 1960s, the lap-lap was standard dress for "town-people." At that time the Awa women and men wore skirts made from bark.

2.

A God Who Controls the Rain

 Guidance results from being
with the Guide.
—Anonymous

IN OUR FIRST FEW MONTHS in Mobuta village, our days were mostly
spent outside our small, windowless dwelling interacting with people.
We cooked outdoors over an open fire. I washed clothes outside in a
small pan set on a pole table with a woven bamboo top. This was a
daily job, as we had brought only one change of clothes each. In plas-
tic buckets, Ed carried water from the local waterfall. The Awas soon
taught him an easier way to do that job. They carried water in a long
bamboo tube that had the inside nodes reamed out. I treated sores
putting on that "wonderful red stuff that stung" (Merthiolate). Since
it stung so badly, it was in the class with their stinging nettle treat-
ments and just had to be good! With a small file, Ed sharpened
knives, spades, machetes, and axes for the people. (Along with the
wash pan and buckets, that file was among those "few essentials" we
had brought with us.) Every interaction we used as an opportunity to
learn more of the beautiful Awa language.

In the fifth month there, Ed enlisted the help of the men as he planned to build a larger house for us. *We'll go back to Ukarumpa and have our baby, then return....* Our next period of six months in the village, we'd live in a more spacious house, one with a door rather than just a doorway with a hanging mat covering it.

What hard workers the Awas are! They chose a site in the middle of the village for our house and helped Ed level it. The men gathered vines and cut trees from the forest. After they skinned the bark from the trees, two men would carry a large pole on their shoulders. Down from the forest they came, chanting, singing, and laughing. Communal work always stirred up a lot of esprit de corps.

Men, women, and children join in thatching a house—Awa style.

The older men judged the suitability of each pole. "No, this pole won't do. It's too soft. Throw it out." Of another they might say, "Termites will eat this pole in the first month. You can't use it." No matter how many times that happened, the pole gatherers did not became discouraged or grow slack in their work. They worked on, not knowing then that Ed planned to reward them later with machetes and knives. Convinced of the superiority of steel over stone, the Awas had already begun to throw their beautifully crafted stone adzes onto the rubbish heap.

The women fanned out over the hillsides where they pulled up strong *kunai* grass for thatch. After beating the dirt from the roots, a woman would carry a huge bundle of grass on her head to the house site. *What a good language-learning experience it would be to go out with the women to get thatch,* I decided. *I can bring back a bundle of grass—maybe not as heavy as they carry, but....*

I got my hat to shade me from the highland sun, put a small bottle of water in a bag, and was ready to go! What fun this would be. But before going, I decided to lift one of the bundles of grass up onto my head. What laughs I got from the women. I couldn't even budge one of those heavy loads, let alone lift it off the ground! "Órétah [their rendition of Aretta], you're still a child now. Wait till you've eaten our sweet potato for a few more months and you'll grow up," I was told.

Because of the hard work the whole village put into the project, we thought we might be able to live a few weeks in our house before returning to Ukarumpa. Alas, the building project slowed down as the rainy season began. The whole community gave a collective shrug of their shoulders knowing that no one could control those heavy tropical rains! But they were to learn that there is—

A God Who Controls the Rain

"Why don't you ask God to 'fasten' the rain?"

That question from some of our Awa friends caught us by surprise. Certainly it would be wonderful if the rain stopped before our trek out to the main road.

We had spent five months living among the Awa. Our plan was that we would stay another month before leaving. But then we received a letter from our director, written five weeks earlier. It read, "I would like you to return to Ukarumpa as soon as possible. I am concerned for Aretta. Hiking on that trail in her condition could be dangerous."

After reading his letter, we told the people we had to leave the next day. The men protested, "The rain is making the trails too slippery for Órétah!" The women urged, "Stay here and give birth to your baby!" Then, holding out hands embedded with garden grime, they offered, "We'll help when your 'uwo, uwo!' time comes."

I held those hands and as graciously as possible declined their offer. I explained that we had been told by "our big-man [our director]" to come. "And we must 'hear his talk [obey him].'"

It was then the men had suggested, "Why don't you ask Jesus to 'fasten' the rain?"

Ask God to *stop* the rain during the rainy season? How could we explain in our faltering Awa that such a request was more than our faith could encompass?

"Well," we said haltingly, "we have asked Jesus to keep it from raining on us while we walk the trail. We'll leave at dawn tomorrow."

That night I worried that maybe we had waited too long to leave the village. *What if I slip and fall on the trail? What if I get heat exhaustion? Or drown in a flooded river? And were we presumptuous to tell the Awas we had asked God to keep it from raining on us? Why, it's been raining every day and every night for the past week! What makes us think...?*

I stopped long enough to listen. "Honey! I don't hear any rain!"

The Lord had led us to pray together and agree in faith that He would hold back the rain while we walked! I dropped to sleep with a prayer on my lips: "Father God, we will trust You to keep me and our baby safe."

The next day at the first streaks of daylight, we left the village. A number of our Awa friends, experts at mountain trekking, came along to help us. We hiked along a narrow ridge. Far below on either side lay fog-filled valleys. Just as we began the 2,000-foot descent to the first rushing river, the sun came out bright and clear, dispelling the fog and drying the trail.

Safely down in the valley, we crossed the river on a swaying vine bridge and began climbing a 1,500-foot ridge. Clouds collected overhead and provided shade from the broiling sun as we plodded upward.

We crested the ridge and walked along it for a couple of hours, then descended again to cross another river.

This time, no bridge—and we noted that the water was higher than usual. But ford that river we must!

We crossed in small groups, gradually working our way across step-by-step. On me, the water was almost chest high; on most of the short Awas, it was more than chest high. Suddenly I saw Manki, a young teenage boy, go under.

"Manki!" I yelled. "I'll save you!"

I dared not move too quickly lest I lose my footing. Manki went under for the second time! One more cautious step and I was able to reach out and grab him by his curly black hair. I lifted a sputtering and coughing boy to safety. By that time, Ed was there to comfort and help. He helped erase tears and saw to it that Manki reached the other shore with no further mishap. Years later Manki became an elder in the village church.

We were safely across. Now more hard climbing faced us.

"Hurry, Órétah, hurry! It's going to rain," the Awas admonished.

"Go on. I'll come slowly," I insisted. "I'm afraid of the big, hot sun."

But go on and leave me? Never! The spirits might find me if I was alone on the trail and beat me, they felt. We all hiked slowly up the side of the last 1,500-foot ridge as the sky turned black and thunder rolled and lightning flashed. It looked like it would pour any minute.

By midafternoon we reached a village. The people there quickly led us to a small thatch dwelling. Grateful that we were safe and dry, we went inside and unrolled sleeping bags. As we dropped down onto them, exhausted, the skies opened and the rain poured!

Snug and dry under the thatch, which Awas cleverly weave to keep out the heavy tropical rains, we talked. "We won't be getting any younger. In years to come, how can we make it in and out of the village over these trails?"

Each morning Ed and I read a psalm together, but since we'd left so early that morning, we'd not yet read for the day. He took out his

King James New Testament, with Psalms in the back, and turned to our reading for the day—Psalm 121.

In the NIV the first verse reads, "I lift up my eyes to the hills—where does my help come from?" We were conscious that indeed our "help comes from the LORD, the Maker of heaven and earth," as the second verse says.

Ed read on. "He will not let your foot slip....the LORD is your shade at your right hand; the sun will not harm you by day.... The LORD will keep you from all harm...." *Well, so much for sunstroke or falling and injuring myself on the trail,* I thought. *But with children will we be able to keep coming in and going out over this trail until we finish this work?* Ed read on, "The LORD will watch over your coming and going both now and forevermore" (Psalm 121:3, 5–8).

No more questions. God had spoken. We knew He would keep me from slipping on the trail and from sunstroke. He would enable us to keep making the trip in and out of the village until we had finished our work among the Awa people.

Dawn brought Christmas day, and with it His peace filled our hearts.

We rested that day, and it rained all day long.

The third day, we hiked again from daybreak till late afternoon. No rain! We rested on the fourth day in another village, and again it rained. By noon the fifth day we reached a government patrol post near the main road. A vehicle was making a mail and grocery run to a small town near Ukarumpa. We accepted the offer of a ride and told our Awa friends goodbye. As the car pulled away, a few drops of rain began to fall. Soon the windshield wipers were frantically whizzing, fighting the pouring rain!

By causing the letter from our director to arrive just when it did, God had guided us to exchange our plans for His. Ed and the Awas had finished the house to a lockable stage; we had slept in it just one night, then left the next day.

And God had answered prayer. He had revealed His power to the Awa people, and He had kept us safe—and dry—on the trail.

PRAYER

God, You are the mighty Creator. You not only created all things, You control all things! You are the perfect Guide. Thank You that when we follow Your plans rather than our own, You bring glory to Yourself!

TO MEDITATE ON

Elijah was a man just like us. He prayed earnestly that it would not rain, and it did not rain on the land for three and a half years. (James 5:17)

The men were amazed and asked, "What kind of man is this? Even the winds and the waves [and the rains] obey him!" (Matthew 8:27)

TO ASK MYSELF

Do I tend to feel that God does miracles for other people but I can't ask Him to do things for me? Or am I aware that He delights in His children and hears their prayers?

3.

Can a Mother Forget
Her Child?

 "Can a mother forget the baby at
her breast and have no compassion
on the child she has borne? Though
she may forget, I will not forget you!
See I have engraved you on the
palms of my hands...."
—Isaiah 49:15–16

OUR FIRST LOVING BABY GIRL was born in the highland town of
Goroka, where the Australian government had established a hospital.
When Karen was three months old, we prepared to return to our village home in Mobuta. We piled our cargo into a group vehicle and
drove to the end of the road. After unloading, we waved goodbye to
our colleague as he drove away. Awa men and women had hiked out
to help us make the two-day trek back to their village. The Awas were
excited to have us return, and all were eager to meet the new baby.

In those first months of Karen's life in the village, I often had
occasion to ponder and appreciate the message of Isaiah 49:15—

Can a Mother Forget Her Child?

Cozily snuggled down into a bark-string bag,[1] three-month-old
Karen was safely carried over the mountains and across three rushing

rivers. We would live with the Awas for six months, this time (we hoped) to continue language learning and to begin telling Bible stories to the two hundred fifty people of Mobuta village. Our ultimate goal was always uppermost in our minds: to translate the New Testament and see lives transformed by reading those life-giving words!

Ed had been adamant that we not give our baby daughter a name that people could tack an "e" sound onto. "No Jeanie, Patty, Suzie names!" he insisted. We both liked the beauty and simplicity of "Karen," and the name seemed safe. But alas! Since no Awa word ends in an *n*, when the Awas met us at the end of the road, they instantly dubbed Karen, "*Iteinahno* Karen-ie! [Our-little-sister Karen!]"

"We want to shake Karenie's hand!" they said.

I cringed. I should have known they would want to greet our baby in their cultural way. Avid hand *shakers* they were, but not great hand *washers*. I could see germs being transferred from Awa-hand to Karen-hand—and then into Karen-mouth. "If you want to greet her, shake her foot," I suggested.

That novel idea took. When people came to Mobuta from other villages, I would hear people telling them, "If you want to shake our little sister's hand, shake her foot." You would have thought the idea originated with the people there in Mobuta!

Late afternoons I often left Karen with her daddy and took leisurely walks, stopping to talk to anyone I met. Many times I would end up at the far end of the village, a long way from home. More than once, my interest captured by some cultural activity, I would forget to look at my watch.

I particularly enjoyed watching a woman, home early from her taro garden, prepare *aboya*. Sitting comfortably on the ground, the woman would first peel taro tubers with a homemade knife: a razor-sharp piece of bamboo. Then with a thorny tree root she would grate the taro. She would add water, and her brown hands would become snow white as they worked the taro-water mixture into a mush. The mush would be spread onto a long, flattened bamboo tube, then bedecked with whatever delicacies the woman had on hand. Smoked rat, smoked frog, or large, white witchetty grubs[2] fresh from the forest were favorites. Finally, the woman would chew up gingerroot and homemade salt, then spew the mixture onto the spread-out mush. She would then roll up the smashed bamboo and stick it inside a still larger bamboo tube. She would lay the larger tube over an open fire and gradually rotate and push it through the fire. The art of cooking *aboya* entails knowing just how long to keep the tube on the fire so that the *aboya* cooks but doesn't burn through the tube. Awa women excel at this art!

Lost in watching such an event, suddenly I would feel my milk surge in. "How could I have forgotten my precious baby girl? She'll be screaming!" I'd berate myself. Dashing madly toward home, I would explain my hurry by calling out, "Karenie *arupibire!* [Karen—her liver is hungry!]"

Mothers sitting in the waning sun nursing their babies would scold, "Yes, go quickly to our little sister!"

An Awa woman often left her baby with a child of seven or eight or with a toothless grandma whose sagging breasts served as a pacifier. After a long day of gardening, she would return late afternoon to a very hungry baby. Yet she never understood a mother who would leave a baby with a husband even for an hour. Females of any age know about babies; husbands don't!

Each time I forgot Karen, I would think of God's question in Isaiah 49:15: "Can a mother forget the baby at her breast and have no compassion on the child she has borne?" And I always agreed with the part of the answer that says, "She may forget!" For I had done it. And done it again. And again.

The answer to that question continues, "Though she may forget, I will not forget you!" That always caused me to rejoice. When I'm feeling neglected by my husband, by my best friend, by coworkers, I take heart in those words spoken long ago to God's people and written for my encouragement today. I rest assured that even though a mother should forget, God says, "I will not forget you!"

PRAYER

Thank You, Father, that I am Your child. Thank You that You are a God who does not forget.

TO MEDITATE ON

Though my father and mother forsake me, the LORD will receive me. (Psalm 27:10)

TO ASK MYSELF

Do I have the assurance that God really does love me and will never, never forsake me? (Read Jeremiah 31:3, John 3:16, Hebrews 13:5.)

---

1. The *bilum*, or bark-string bag as I've called it throughout this book, is a loose-netted bag woven from strands of bark, hand rolled by women on bare thighs. A female carries her *bilum* slung over her head. Heavy loads of sweet potato and other root crops are carried in a *bilum*. Babies, also, ride in a *bilum* slung over their mother's head. I've never known a woman to drop a baby carried in a *bilum*.
2. Witchetty grubs are large white larva of any of several species of moth and beetle that live in decaying wood. The Awa consider these grubs, raw or cooked, a delicacy.

4.

Whirlpools of Worry

 Trust in the Lord with all your heart and lean not on your own understanding; in all your ways acknowledge him....
—Proverbs 3:5–6

"I can't trust and worry at the same time—can I?"
—Ariana, a Janette Oke fictional heroine

THE AWA WOMAN'S THREE greatest delights in life are her children, her gardens, and her pigs. Though I tended no garden, nor did I own pigs, I did have children. I soon learned that Karen and Treesa were my credentials for acceptance by the Awas as a real woman. In those first years of living among the Awas, my daughters were my greatest asset in establishing deep relationships with the women. Conversation about pregnancy, childbirth, and children in general gave us an area of common ground. Still there was a great gulf between us.

The Awa women had many fears. Fears that I could not relate to. Unlike them, I did not fear the spirits. I knew the divine Spirit, who "is greater than the one in the world" (1 John 4:4). I did not have to worry about a dry season that would dry up the gardens, leaving my family short of food. We had a small cache of food—and we could always leave and return to the Ukarumpa center.

The Awa women's worst fear, a "pay-back"[1] killing that would leave their children without a father, I did not even consider a possibility. I did, however, occasionally think about *other* things that could happen and leave me a widow and leave Karen and Treesa without a father. What would I do way out here, far away from anybody if my husband died or was accidentally killed? Karen was three years old, Treesa was eighteen months old when that thinking grew into a swirling worry. I felt I was being sucked under by—

Whirlpools of Worry

"Tautau wánine! Sahri aiq taqnobagire!"

The jungle grapevine, activated by women who had left with their bark-string fishnets early that morning, relayed the message up the 2,000-foot incline to the village: "Angry, red river! Bridge gone!"

Six months had elapsed since the floods had swept away the main link to the outside world. It was the dry season, the time to replace that swinging vine bridge. Awa men are expert builders with jungle materials. Their bamboo and vine bridges span 100 feet or more above rushing mountain rivers.

It was 1963. Living in the village, we were translating the Gospel of Mark into Awa. The two-day hike into and out of Awaland entailed crossing rivers over swinging vine bridges.

Ed was going down to the river with the Awa men to help choose a site for the new bridge. That I'd be alone all day in the village with our two small daughters wasn't my main concern. That was minor compared to my major problem.

The past few weeks I'd been nearly sucked under by worry. Ed would go on a firewood foray with the men, and I'd visualize an ax head flying off the ax handle and hitting him in the head. Or he'd join the men on a hunt, and I'd see one of those pig-killing arrows missing its intended mark. When I wasn't conjuring up such unlikely accidents, I could stimulate my overactive imagination with various illnesses—everything from malaria to a common heart attack.

I knew Philippians 4:6 commanded me not to worry about anything but in everything by prayer with thanksgiving to make my requests known to God. The next verse promised that "the peace of God" would guard my heart and mind. But it wasn't working. I would pray and confess my worry as sin and ask forgiveness. Two days later, all peace would be gone, again replaced by worry and fear.

Now it was the night before Ed's trip. I knew the real danger of that river; tales abounded of Awas swept away, their bodies never recovered. After we'd blown out our tiny wick lantern, I lay in the dark, tense and tormented. *I may never see even his body again.* I reached over and touched my husband.

"Having trouble getting to sleep, Honey?" he asked.

"Yes. I'm...aaaa...I'm worried," I confessed. Then all I'd tried so hard to handle alone with God tumbled out—the past weeks of frustration and fear.

"I had no idea. Why didn't you tell me? Let's pray," he said.

The next morning I waved goodbye to Ed and the Awas, still aware of the deep peace that had flooded my heart after we had prayed the night before. The peace remained through a busy morning: handing out malaria medication, giving a penicillin shot for a yaws sore,[2] treating minor cuts and sores—all interspersed with chatting about children, gardens, and pigs!

"This is a good afternoon to visit Old Granny," I told the girls after they awoke from their naps. Older Awa kids were all too willing to piggyback our girls up the steep mountain paths. Beautiful soft black hair made a nice pillow for the girls to lay their heads on. So the mention of a visit to Old Granny was met with squeals of delight by Karen and Treesa.

Old Granny had married into a clan of the Mobuta village but still retained her other-village accent. That, plus my imperfect Awa made communication with her difficult. I longed to tell her Bible stories we had translated. A teenage boy came along to translate my stumbling phrases into good Awa.

In the midst of our joint effort to tell Granny Bible stories, I looked at my watch. Three o'clock already! I remembered Ed and felt a pleasant pang of guilt. Not only had I not worried, I had not even thought about him all day long. And here it was midafternoon.

I lifted my heart to God. "Thank You, Father! I've not worried about my husband today."

Shortly before dark, Ed, looking somewhat bedraggled, and the Awas, loud and enthusiastic as usual, returned. "How was your day?" I greeted my husband.

"Good," he replied with a sheepish grin, " 'cept I lost my hat."

"Oh, I'm sorry!" The tone of my voice belied my words. Ed knew I disliked that hat—a relic of the Australian army. "How did you lose it?"

"It disappeared when I was in the whirlpool," he replied, trying to sound nonchalant, as though he spent time in whirlpools every day.

"I made it. But little boy Tukiro didn't!"

"I leaped across that place where the river rushes between those two huge boulders. You know, the place that always scares you so much. All the men followed me, then Tukiro tried to jump across. But his little-boy legs didn't quite make it. I had gone downstream, just in case. I jumped in and snatched Tukiro just as the torrent was about to sweep him past me.

"I tried to fight my way back to shore, but I was no match for that current. It swept us downstream, where we tumbled over a small waterfall. That part was sorta fun!" my fun-loving husband interjected. "However, the river turned into a huge whirlpool. We were carried around and under, around and under...."

Listening to my husband, I felt like crying. But it was *him* standing here before me. "Go on," I gulped.

"I was hanging on to Tukiro by an arm, no longer able to keep his head above water. He felt as limp as one of those plucked chickens we used to sell back on the farm. Fighting to keep from being sucked into the eye of that monster, I lost track of the times it pulled us under. Each time we'd surface, I'd try to find a niche in the bank to grab, but it was sheer rock cliff, slimy with moss.

"I knew that I needed both arms free to have a hope of getting out. But the ever so slim chance that Tukiro might not have become just a body caused me to hang on to him.

"What a relief to look up and see the men lowering one of the teenage boys down the cliff by his ankles. On one circle around I lifted Tukiro's arm up, and the boy grabbed him. Only then was I able to swim free.

"And guess what? When I climbed out, there sat Tukiro, minus his G-string, but very much alive!" Grinning, he added, "And I'm very much alive, too, though minus your favorite hat!"

We laughed together at his joke. Or were we laughing to relieve the tension?

"What time did this all happen?" I asked, even though I knew the answer.

"Oh, midafternoon sometime. Around three o'clock, I'd reckon."

The past few weeks I, too, had fought a whirlpool. No, not just one whirlpool but dozens of whirlpools. Whirlpools of worry. Now I also was very much alive—free from the vicious grip of worry that had sought to drown me spiritually. Prayer and thanksgiving had freed me.

PRAYER

Lord God, I am aware that no one "by worrying can add a single hour to his life" (Matthew 6:27) or to the life of a loved one. Thank You for Your peace when we cast our worries on You!

TO MEDITATE ON

Cast all your anxiety on him because he cares for you. (1 Peter 5:7)

Don't give in to worry.... It only leads to trouble. (Psalm 37:8 TEV)

Therefore confess your sins [worry] to each other and pray for each other so that you may be healed. The prayer of a righteous man is powerful and effective. (James 5:16)

TO ASK MYSELF

E. Stanley Jones[3] tells of a man who had a "Worry Tree" in his front yard. Before he came into the house, the man hung his worries on that tree. Jones concludes, "For the Christian that 'Worry Tree' is the cross." Do I hang my worries on the cross? If for any reason I'm unable to do that on my own, do I seek out someone to pray with me and help me do so?

---

1. "Pay-back" permeates the Papua New Guinea culture. When one group believes there must be retribution, often it is an innocent person who becomes the victim of pay-back. Only the power of the gospel has proven effective to break the endless chain of pay-back!
2. Yaws is an infectious contagious tropical disease marked by ulcerating lesions that can eat into the bone if left untreated. A yaws sore responds dramatically to penicillin.
3. *Abundant Living,* E. Stanley Jones, 1982, Nashville: Abington.

5.

"Don't Do Dat!"

 When the devil starts tampering
with you, dare to resist him....
our God loves that kind of
courage among His people.
—A. W. Tozer

OUR SECOND DAUGHTER, Treesa, born when Karen was eighteen months old, was our sunny happy-heart, a child who always seemed to have a heart bigger than her tiny build.

"Mommy, can I give my tennis shoes to Jeanie?"

"Do you have *two* pairs, Treesa?"

"No, but Jeanie doesn't have any at all."

To Treesa it wasn't important that she wouldn't have a pair of tennis shoes if she gave hers to Jeanie. The important thing was that Jeanie didn't have a pair!

Treesa threw herself wholeheartedly into everything she did. She never saw anything she wanted to accomplish as an impossibility. A "let's move on and get this done" type of little girl, she took charge of the situation and organized her peers to move with her! That was our delightful second-born.

Today Treesa is a godly woman, married, with two beautiful daughters and a good-looking son (an admittedly biased grandmother's opinion). She and her husband, Michael Hause, live in Manila and teach at Faith Academy, a school for missionaries' children (we affectionately call them MKs—missionary kids).

Long ago I learned from Treesa not to let circumstances control me, but to control them. I learned that I could look adversity in the face and say—

"Don't Do Dat!"

One day while playing in the yard, our trusting three-year-old Treesa was showing excessive interest in a brood of newly hatched balls of fluff and peep on spindly legs. That interest led her too close to clucking Mother Hen, who, feeling her brood was being threatened, flew at her. The result: Tears mingled with blood cascaded down cheeks made rosy by the tropical highland sun. That same week, a bee stung Treesa on her arm. Again tears, but also a little girl wiser about the ways of chickens and bees.

True to her nature, Treesa was not about to give in to circumstances! She took the situation in hand. She was ready to confront every chicken that strutted about and every bee that flew into our yard. She would look them in the eye (as best one can look a chicken or a bee in the eye) and with a seasoned three-year-old air of authority command, "Don't do dat!"

Minor annoyances and irritations. Adverse circumstances. An attack from the enemy. They come to discourage us, to overwhelm us, to devour us. With an air of authority that comes from the One who has all power in heaven and on earth, we can face those things, we can face our enemy and say, "Don't do dat!"

PRAYER

God, grant that I will be strong and not just give in to circumstances. Grant me wisdom to resist the devil.

TO MEDITATE ON

Stand your ground....Throw yourselves into the work of the Master, confident that nothing you do for him is a waste of time or effort. (1 Corinthians 15:58 *The Message*)

Submit yourselves, then, to God. Resist the devil, and he will flee from you. (James 4:7)

TO ASK MYSELF

Under adverse circumstances do I give up? Or do I, like Treesa, look things squarely in the eye and with God's enabling take charge of the situation? Do I obey God's command to resist the enemy and experience him fleeing from me?

6.

That Hanging-Upside-Down Feeling

 Although the threads of my life have often seemed knotted, I know, by faith, that on the other side of the embroidery there is a crown.
—Corrie ten Boom

WHAT IS THAT NOISE in Treesa's bedroom? I cautiously opened her door. Thwang! Thwang! Huge moths and butterflies, trapped behind the louvered windows, frantically thrashed about hitting against the wire screen.

How like our eight-year-old Treesa! Last week she scavenged for cocoons; this week her room resembles a butterfly farm.

Anything that moves or will move, watch out, or Treesa will get you!

Treesa even collected things that *didn't* move.

I turned to check her desk. Had she thrown away those tiny sticks when she cleaned her room yesterday? No, they were still there—and marching all over her desk! That was my first encounter with the stick insect!*

In PNG, our girls enjoyed a variety of pets. New Guinea opossums, wallabies, sugar-gliders, parrots, cockatoos, guinea pigs—and, of course, puppies and kittens. If Treesa's collections of butterflies and moths, stick insects, rhinoceros and elephant beetles, green and blue beetles, praying mantises, spiders of all sorts and sizes, plus a myriad of unnamed insects, counted as pets, the list would be much longer!

Years ago, when we were at our Ukarumpa center awaiting Treesa's birth, we felt that Karen was too young to have a pet. Nevertheless, two kittens made their way into our hearts and home and quickly became more precious to our Karen than her doll.

One sunny day Karen's interaction with her two pets reminded me that God always holds me in His hand, even when I am experiencing—

That Hanging-Upside-Down Feeling

The pathetic cries, "Meow! Meow! Meow!" grew louder and more intense. Our eighteen-month-old toddler was outside playing with her two tiny pets. Sitting at my desk doing language analysis, I ignored the cries of terror as long as possible without endangering the very life of the kittens. Finally I jumped up and ran outside. *What new form of kitty torture is Karen innocently inflicting on those tiny creatures?* I wondered. I had repeatedly instructed Karen that "if Kitty meows when you're holding him, quickly let him go, because that's Kitty's way of saying, 'You're hurting me!'"

Karen was nonchalantly walking up the path toward me. In one hand she carried one of her kittens in what must have seemed to her baby mind a most appropriate fashion: by his "handle"—his tail—upside down. She stopped, looked up at me, and flashed one of those cherub smiles designed to melt a mother's heart.

The pitiful cries of "Meow! Meow!" did not cease. About to reprimand her by yelling, "Karen Elizabeth! What *are* you doing?" I noticed that Kitty-Held-by-the-Tail was quietly hanging in perfect peace and acceptance. He even wore a kitty grin on his upside-down face. Or so I imagined.

Karen stood in the bright sunshine, smiling angelically as she looked up at me, still holding Kitty in this most unorthodox way.

Upside-down Kitty was not making a sound. Rather, Baby Brother Kitten, trailing behind and ignored by his mistress, was responsible for the pathetic meowing that had torn me from my desk.

What could I say? I merely smiled back at my darling. Then, endeavoring to explain my sudden appearance, I mumbled something noncommittal like, "Hi, Sweetie. Mommy just came to see what her girl was doing."

I then turned and went back inside to ponder what I had just seen.

How often when undergoing some trial do I feel that I, like Kitty, am hanging upside down? But do I react as calmly and submissively as Kitty did? Or do I scream and cry out with grumbling, complaining, and questioning?

Baby Brother Kitten, running behind, had good reason to cry; he had been totally ignored. Don't we find a parallel in the spiritual realm? "It is for discipline that you have to endure.... For what son is there whom his father does not discipline? If you are left without discipline...you are illegitimate children and not sons..." (Hebrews 12:7–8 RSV).

The kitten in Karen's hand was being held—and held firmly. No matter that he was hanging upside down. He was being held securely; he was not being ignored.

My Christian life is not always smooth and calm, without trials. I sometimes feel confused and mixed up, as if I were hanging upside down. But I'm reminded that whatever trial I go through, however confused and mixed up I am, how upside down I feel, I am in my Savior's hand; I am held firmly and securely by the One who said, "I give them eternal life, and they shall never perish; no one can snatch them out of my hand" (John 10:28). Let me cry out only if my Lord ceases to hold me. And, O glorious truth, He never will!

PRAYER

Lord, in the trials and testings You allow to come into my life, I experience Your loving care. Thank You that You never ignore me, that You hold me securely.

TO MEDITATE ON

I give them eternal life, and they shall never perish; no one can snatch them out of my hand. (John 10:28)

Blessed is the man you discipline, O LORD, the man you teach from your law. (Psalm 94:12)

TO ASK MYSELF

When I feel like I'm hanging upside down, what is my reaction? Do I trust God, who said, "For I know the plans I have for you,...plans to prosper you and not to harm you, plans to give you hope and a future" (Jeremiah 29:11)?

---

* See Appendix E.

7·

A Nap Taker's Creed

> Just as a woman knows she's a mother because of that special bond between her and a certain child, the key to knowing I'm a Christian is that unique bond between [me] and my Savior.
> —Sheryl Haystead

UKARUMPA, THE MAIN administrative center in Papua New Guinea, lies in the beautiful Aiyura Valley of PNG's highlands. In the 1960s and 1970s, after living three to five months in Mobuta village with the Awas, we would come to Ukarumpa for a few weeks or months— to participate in linguistic or translation workshops; to have babies; to get Scripture books printed; or later, after our daughters were in school, to be with them during school vacations.

Lex and Val Collier were a support couple from Australia who lived at Ukarumpa, serving in Bible translation by helping where their skills fitted. Val, as center hostess, made sure that new people, guests, and translators coming in from villages felt welcome and were assigned a house to live in. Lex, a mechanic, trained and supervised Papua New Guinea men. Lex and these men kept our group-owned jeep running—as well as a World War II vintage vehicle could be kept running, that is.

49

When Ed and I first went out to live with the Awas in Mobuta village, all thirty or so of our Ukarumpa coworkers gathered at dawn by the loaded jeep to pray us off. The amen! was said, and Ed, Lex, and I climbed in. Ed turned the key and was rewarded with a grinding sound. Lex got out and raised the hood. For the next ten minutes he tinkered with whatever it is that mechanics tinker with. Still the jeep wouldn't start. Next Lex got under the jeep.

One by one the crowd drifted homeward for breakfast. Forty-five minutes later, only Lex, Ed, and I were still there. Lex's magic touch finally got the old jeep going, and away we went to the end of the road, a mere sixty miles that stretched over six long hours. Each time we came to a stream (and it seemed like there were hundreds of them), Ed stopped, and he or Lex checked out the pole decking of the bridge. It wouldn't do for a wheel to drop into a hole because of rotted poles.

The trek in over the mountains wasn't easy.

At some hills, Lex and I got out and followed while Ed drove up steep, slippery inclines. Sometimes, we even unloaded some of the cargo and carried it up the hill.

With a sigh of relief, we reached the end of the road. After we unloaded the vehicle, we waved goodbye to Lex as he drove away, wending his way back to Ukarumpa. "Lord, help him to make it back before nightfall without more jeep mishaps."

The trek in over the mountains wasn't easy, but still it was less stressful than the uncertainties raised by slick roads, rotting pole bridges, and the unreliability of World War II jeeps. Besides all that, we sometimes felt like churned butter once we arrived at the end of the road. It was always a joy to be met there by Awa men and women who came out to help us over the formidable mountain paths.

In the following ten years, before our group had a helicopter, Lex made that trip to the end of the road with us a number of times. We became fast friends with the Collier family. Both Lex and Val were hard workers, and come Sunday afternoon, they felt the need for a little snooze.

Their daughter Josie wondered about that and seemed to have formulated in her mind—

A Nap Taker's Creed

"Daddy," six-year-old Josie asked her father, "are people who don't take naps on Sunday afternoon Christians?"

Josie had observed that her parents always took a Sunday afternoon nap and that they were Christians. Therefore, she reasoned, the opposite must be true: Some people don't take Sunday afternoon naps; those people must not be Christians.

We laugh at a six-year-old's naiveté. But often we ask the same question, substituting our own list of taboos for "don't take naps on Sunday afternoon." "Are people who don't do this or who do that really Christians?" we ask, perhaps not verbally but in silent judgment.

Yet how simple is God's definition of the one who is a Christian, the one who has life. It's the person who has Jesus living within: "He who has the Son has life; he who does not have the Son of God does not have life" (1 John 5:12).

No, a person is not a Christian because he or she abstains from certain things. Likewise a person is not a Christian because he or she does certain things. Tozer reminds us in *Man: The Dwelling Place of God* that "baptism, confirmation, the receiving of the sacraments, church membership—these mean nothing unless the supreme act of God in regeneration also takes place."

And the apostle Paul reminds us in words easier to comprehend that "if anyone does not have the Spirit of Christ, he does not belong to Christ" (Romans 8:9b).

No, Josie, it's neither those who take naps nor those who don't take naps....

PRAYER

Thank You, Father, for salvation through Jesus, Your *gift* to us.

TO MEDITATE ON

But when the kindness and love of God our Savior appeared, he saved us, not because of righteous things we had done, but because of his mercy. He saved us through the washing of rebirth and renewal by the Holy Spirit. (Titus 3:4–5)

TO ASK MYSELF

Do I have a do-this and don't-do-that list that I apply as a criterion for salvation? Or do I realize that salvation is a gift from God and that nothing a person does can earn eternal life?

8.

Obedience Is Better

The route to fulfillment is not the one with the road sign reading "Pleasures Ahead" or "If it seems to meet your needs, keep going." The only sure path to real and lasting joy is the steep, rugged road marked "Obedience."
—Lawrence Crabb, Jr.

IN THE VILLAGE WE HAD LIVED in a thatch-roofed house with woven bamboo walls and screenless windows. When we came to the Ukarumpa Center, we lived in an aluminum-roofed house with Sheetrock walls and louvered glass windows.

Right down the hill, within "a cuppa-sugar borrowing" distance, lived another support couple from Australia, the Mileses. Like Lex, Bill Miles was a mechanic and helped train and supervise PNG mechanics. His wife, Helen, served as our post office administrator making sure letters and packages from home were put in the right slot for each person.

Bill and Helen had three children. Their five-year-old David was all boy! His freckle-faced smile could have charmed a death adder had the Aiyura Valley been home to such poisonous snakes, as is the Awa village in which we had lived and worked.

I wouldn't have exactly compared David to a bull in a china shop, but I might have likened him to a kangaroo in an egg-packing house. Even so, God used him to remind me that—

Obedience Is Better

The pungent smell of fresh paint wafted through my kitchen window. As I washed dishes that morning, I looked out to once again admire my artwork glistening in the sun. Our back porch handrails now seemed to stand straighter and taller, as though they shared my feeling of pride over their new coat of paint.

Then I saw him. Oh, no! Our five-year-old neighbor was headed straight for the back porch—and those freshly painted handrails.

"Come around to the front door, David," I hollered. "There's wet paint on the porch rails."

"I'll be careful," David calmly assured me, scrunching his shoulders inward and continuing toward the steps.

"No, David! Don't come up those steps," I called out sternly. The steps were narrow, and I knew all too well this young dynamo's attempts at carefulness. Last week he had walked on our glass window louvers, which I had washed and laid out on the lawn to dry. I can't explain it, but the louvers hadn't broken. I suspect that if angels were paid overtime, David's heavenly guardian would net a fat check each month.

"I'll be careful," David said again, oblivious to my concern and now dangerously close to the steps.

"David, stop!" I yelled. "I don't want *carefulness*. I want *obedience*!"

As those words burst from my mouth, I remembered Samuel's rebuke to Saul in 1 Samuel 15. Saul had disobeyed God after God had clearly told him, "Now go, attack the Amalekites and totally destroy everything that belongs to them. Do not spare them;..." (v.3a).

"But Saul and the army spared Agag [the king of the Amalekites] and the best of the sheep and cattle, the fat calves and lambs—everything that was good" (v. 9a).

Later, after greeting Samuel with what seems to be a religious cliché, Saul twice boasted that he had done exactly what the Lord had told him to do. "The LORD bless you! I have carried out the LORD's instructions," he said (v. 13b).

Saul tried to justify his actions by blaming the soldiers, even attributing a religious motive to his disobedience: "The soldiers... spared the best of the sheep and cattle to sacrifice to the LORD your God..." (v. 15).

It was after Saul had repeated his "blame speech" (v. 21) that Samuel rebuked him. "Does the LORD delight in burnt offerings and sacrifices as much as in obeying the voice of the LORD? To obey is better than sacrifice...." (v. 22).

Now as I yelled out to David, those words of Samuel echoed in my mind: "To obey is better than sacrifice."

David's reply to my harsh command "I don't want carefulness. I want obedience!" melted my sternness. "All right, Loving," he cheerfully conceded, flashing one of his winning smiles at me. "I'll go around to the front door."

My young neighbor's obedience, his cherubic smile, and his special name for me—no one else called me by my last name—made me forget how impish and careless he could be.

As I went to the front door to let David in, I thought, *How often am I like Saul or David, wanting to go my own way?* "Lord, I'll be careful," I rationalize as I proceed with my plans. Like Saul, I may even try to blame others for my disobedience. Saul blamed the soldiers; I may blame my husband or my children or my neighbor. I can always find someone to blame if I'm trying to excuse my sin.

I may even try to justify my waywardness on a religious platform, proclaiming to myself (who else would be fooled?) that some good for the Lord will come out of this.

How glad I am that God at such times firmly calls to me in a still, small voice. "Aretta, stop! I don't want your carefulness; I don't want your sacrifices. I want your obedience!"

PRAYER

Lord, whenever You find me with my shoulders scrunched inward trailblazing rather than following Your way, stop me. Help me to hear Your voice and to change direction as quickly and cheerfully as David did.

TO MEDITATE ON

Whoever has my commands and obeys them, he is the one who loves me. He who loves me will be loved by my Father, and I too will love him and show myself to him. (John 14:21)

TO ASK MYSELF

Am I walking on a path I myself have chosen as I rationalize, "I'll be careful"? Is it possible that I am even walking on a path clearly marked in His Word as a "thou shalt not" path?

9.

The Old Ones

 A wise man thinks much of death,
while the fool thinks only of having
a good time.
—Ecclesiastes 7:4 TLB

THE NARROW OPENING of the small, round house was barricaded with lengths of bamboo. The barricade shut out the chill of the highlands night; it also ensured that no *wahnsa* would enter and inflict illness on Kanah and her children.

Earlier in the evening Kanah's husband had come down from the "men's house." He sat cross-legged in the uphill half of his wife's house—the half reserved for his use. Without comment, he took the sweet potato Kanah handed him. Young Mowani, his eyes propped open only by prongs of hunger, watched his father eat. As soon as his father finished and went back uphill to sleep, he and his little sister would eat. Then....

Where am I? Mowani wondered. A shaft of morning sunlight shone through a crack in the woven bamboo wall causing him to close his eyes again.

Had he finished his sweet potato last night before he fell asleep? The warmth of the fire, the softness of Kanah's body—those were the last things he remembered. But he knew Kanah's strong arms had lifted him and placed him on their sleeping mat. There he and his little sister slept, snuggled close against Kanah, their mother. The fire turned to ashes, and fingers of fog crept through the cracks in the walls and penetrated the large bark cape covering them. Mowani shivered and moved closer to Kanah's warm body.

Now it was morning, a new day bathed in moist, mountain air waiting to be dried by the tropical sunlight.

In the early months, when learning the Awa language was our main focus, Ed and I sat many an evening with a family in the wife's house. Ed was always careful to sit on the uphill side of the house with the husband. The "players" were different, but the drama was usually the same: hungry children uncomplainingly waiting their turn to eat, often falling asleep before they finished their sweet potato meal.

This scenario provided a cultural illustration that "shot the liver [really got the attention]" of Old-Man-Yehma, one of—

The Old Ones

As I lay on my bed staring up at the thatch roof of our village house, hot, angry tears spilled onto my pillow. I was angry at my husband, angry at myself. Old people in the village were dying without believing in Jesus, and I was upset.

Maybe if Ed had involved more old people in the Awa translation work; maybe if we had spent more time sitting in their smoky houses talking with them about their pigs, their gardens, their children, the fighting days of long ago—things they loved to talk about. If only I had been more patient, more loving.

I tortured myself with "if onlys" and "maybe ifs." I ranted inwardly—at Ed, at myself, even at God.

"God, You could cause these old people to believe. They're dying and going into eternity without knowing Christ. These are people I know, people I love. Don't You care that I hurt because these people are dying without believing?" I complained.

"Why do my questions always meet with silence from You, God? Can't You answer me? Today Ume-Old-Woman died. Last week I visited her and tried to tell her about You as she sat in the sun warming herself. '*Maniká, Maniká, Maniká.* That's all you talk about! I don't want to hear any more about Him!' she spat out, then turned her back on me."

Finally, exhausted from self-pity, I whispered, "Don't You care, God? Don't You care?" But this time my question was different. It was a plea not for my hurt but for the salvation of the old men and women of the village still living.

"Yes, I care," the Father's gentle voice seemed to speak deep within me. "You are suffering over these few that you know and love. But I knew and loved their fathers, their grandfathers, and their great-grandfathers.... I sent My beloved Son to die for them."

Humbled, I could only whisper, "Lord, forgive me for doubting Your love. I know You love these old ones, and You've suffered through the ages as people have died without turning to You. Thank You for the privilege of bearing just a small part of Your suffering now."

Our work went on: language learning, making primers so that people could learn to read, training teachers, and translating with the help of young men who had become believers. Eventually, some of the old ones also "put truth to [believed in]" Jesus.

One day Yehma-Old-Man was helping me check translation. Someone in the village had recently died.

"Aretta-Old-Woman," Yehma addressed me with a title of respect, "we black people are very afraid to die. Are *red* people afraid to die, too?"

"Some are, Yehma-Old-Man; some aren't. Those who don't have Jesus living in their livers are afraid to die—unless they're foolish and never think about dying. But those who have put truth to Jesus and walk His trail are not afraid to die."

Yehma seemed to be thinking deeply about what I'd told him.

Lord, help me. Give me wisdom and the right Awa words to talk to him, I prayed silently.

"Yehma, remember when you were a little boy and in the cold evenings sat by the warm fire your mother had built? You'd fall asleep leaning against her. The next morning you'd awaken—not lying by the fire, but on your sleeping mat in the corner. You didn't remember when your mother picked you up and put you on your bed the night before."

As the scene of long ago played across Yehma's memory, he smiled and grunted, "Um-mmmm."

"That's how death is for those who have put truth to Jesus. We 'fall asleep' here on earth, then God picks us up in His strong arms and takes us to His Good Garden. So, Yehma-Old-Man, put truth to Jesus," I urged. "He will then 'not put your sins on his ears [forgive you].' His blood that flowed down when evil men stuck Him on the tree will make you as white as the cockatoo's feathers. And you won't be afraid to die because you'll go to God's Beautiful Garden!"

This time no grunt from Yehma. Had he understood my illustration, my urging him to believe in Jesus? *Lord, help him understand even if my use of the Awa language is far from perfect,* I prayed.

A few weeks later as we were leaving the village for furlough, Yehma clasped my hands and bid me goodbye. "Pray that I'll not die while you're gone," he said.

"I will," I told him. "But if you are dying, remember what I told you."

Yehma threw back his head and laughed. His dark eyes sparkled. He turned to the man standing next to him. "She says we don't have to be afraid to die if we put truth to Jesus. Dying is like falling asleep by the fire and waking up in God's Beautiful Garden."

Dear old man, you did understand! My words "shot your liver," my heart sang.

Yehma was there when we returned from our furlough. He came to the meetings to hear the young men teach from the translated

Scriptures. We were away from the village when he died. Amah, his wife, reported that before dying he told her, "I'm going to wake up in God's Beautiful Garden."

Then there was Ehni-Old-Man. He, too, came to hear God's Word expounded. Before he died, Ehni told his family and friends, "I used to wonder, *Is the Talk true or is it not true?* Now I know it *is* true. I'm going to leave you and go to God's Beautiful Garden. Don't wail and mourn for me."

As Ehni lay dying, he had a vision of a crossroad. One way led down to a place of fire, the other up to a lovely garden. Jesus stood at the uphill fork calling, "Come!" After exhorting his wife to "walk behind Jesus on God's trail," Ehni died peacefully.

"Those who sow in tears will reap with songs of joy. He who goes out weeping, carrying seed to sow, will return with songs of joy, carrying sheaves with him" (Psalm 126:5–6). Our gracious Father God takes note of our tears—yes, even our angry ones, if we bring them to Him.

PRAYER

Thank You, God, that You love each one of us. Thank You that there will be people from every language group in Your "Beautiful Garden."

TO MEDITATE ON

[The Lord] will swallow up death forever.... (Isaiah 26:8 TLB)

But as for me, my contentment is...in seeing you and knowing all is well between us. And when I awake in heaven, I will be fully satisfied, for I will see you face to face. (Psalm 17:15 TLB)

TO ASK MYSELF

Am I concerned about people's eternal destination? Do I try to play God in the lives of some whom I love and long to see come to Him? Or do I remember that salvation is of the Lord?

10.

Questions, Questions, Questions!

 "What did you do when you felt like giving up?"

No one [on the missionary panel] spoke for almost a minute. Then a man who had been a missionary for over 40 years, who had faced and escaped from a firing squad during a fearful civil war in Africa, replied: "Giving up was never an option. We never considered it—we *knew* we were where God wanted us."

—David Morley

"HOW DO THEY BREATHE?!"

On our first furlough, photo album pictures of Awa grooms sporting large, white "wedding rings"—pig tusks worn in a hole through their noses—brought forth this most frequently asked question.

"Aaaa...well, we never thought about it. But they *do* breathe. After they eat, they take the pig tusks out of their belts where they had stuck them, lick them so they'll easily slide back into their...."

Uh, oh! The look on the face of our hostess clued us that we had already told more than she wanted to know.

"What do you eat in New Guinea?" was a close contestant for first place.

That was easier, and safer, to answer: "Anthropologically, the Awa are called *subsistence farmers*. Sweet potato is the Awa staple. Besides growing more than fifteen types of sweet potato, they grow a variety

An Awa groom with his "wedding ring" through his nose.

of other root crops: taro, yam, cassava, wingbean potatoes. We eat lots of these root crops. We also eat corn, beans, green leafy vegetables, and peanuts.

"The Awa are classified as 'hunters and gatherers.' They set traps in the forest to catch marsupials, wild pigs, and cassowaries. In the grasslands they hunt for bandicoots and field rats. The women warn me, 'Aretta, you must not eat rat! It's taboo for women.'

"I promise with great glee, 'I won't!'

"We're never offered *kaskas* (an opossumlike animal from the forest), since obligatory gift exchanges dictate that the *kaskas* be given to in-laws. Occasionally someone shoots a wild pig in the forest or kills a domestic pig and brings us pork. No trichinosis in New Guinea! Our first time living in Mobuta, we allotted ourselves only one can of meat a week from the cache of food we had brought with us. We'd practically fight over who got the privilege of licking the lid of the can!

"We missed fruit. Awa children brought wild strawberries from the grasslands. Their parents thought we were crazy. '*Íre nah nanere!* [Totally inedible!]' they would scornfully declare. Fortunately, the small sugar banana grew in abundance. Later we brought in pineapple shoots. And banana plants that grew Chiquita-like fruit (well, almost!) for people to plant in their gardens. They also planted papaya seed we gave them, and in a year or two the trees yielded fruit."

"How did you ever learn that language with no books to help you?" was near the top of the ten most frequently asked questions.

On this subject we could really hold forth. We had such fun learning Awa monolingually. Yes, not only no books but also no writing system, no common language in which to communicate. The Awa people knew no English, not even Pidgin English. We could not say, "In your language, how do you say...?" However, a compensating factor was a whole village of language experts of all ages eager to teach us.

We learned the language by asking—

Questions, Questions, Questions!

One question we could easily pantomime: We pointed to ask, "What is that?" The Awa people understood our "pointed question" (pun intended) and responded by giving the name of the pointed-at object. It was several weeks before we stumbled onto the much-longed-for phrase "What is that?" I pointed at the leafy greens I was preparing to stuff into a bamboo tube and cook over our outdoor fire. I directed my point to a man on the other side of the fire. The man hesitated, then said, "*Anepomo.*"

"*Taraq*," a man sitting next to him said.

Oh, no, I thought, *two words for these greens? And that other word ends in a glottal stop.*[1]

So I ignored *taraq* and repeated ever so carefully, "*A-ne-po-mo.*"

The first man leaned toward me. "*Taraq*," he said.

Now why, I wondered, *did he change his mind? He first said anepomo, now this other word. Well, that second word's just too hard to say!*

"*Anepomo*," I said again as I pointed at the greens.

He leaned closer. "*Taraq! Taraq!*" he yelled.

Then it registered! I had just learned to say, "What is that?" The first man must have temporarily forgotten the name of the greens. He had turned to the man beside him and asked, "What is that? [*Anepomo.*]"[2]

I pointed at several things for which I already knew the names and said, "*Anepomo.*" Someone responded with the right name every time!

Ed was inside taking a nap on our now leveled bed. I dashed inside and woke him to share my wonderful news.

"So you think you know how to say, 'What is that?'" my skeptical husband teased. "When you tried it, did you point?"

Yes, I admitted, I had pointed.

"Well, these people are conditioned by pointing like Pavlov's dogs were conditioned by the bell. If you pointed at something and said *Abracadabra*, they'd come back with the right answer."

"All right, let's go outside and try it!"

Outside, I pointed to man's best friend in Awaland: his pig. Always plenty of those wandering around. "*Abracadabra*," I said to the pig's *abowá* [father, hence also owner].

The owner's eyes widened. He turned to someone nearby and said something I didn't understand. *Did he say, "What's gotten into her anyway?"*

I repeated my performance, pointing to the ground, a tree, a dog. Each time the response was much the same. Then I switched to "*Anepomo*." Each person asked responded with the correct name. We now could verbalize our first question!

We sat on the ground with our neighbors, scratching fleabites with the best of them, and listened, pointed, repeated. More listening, more repeating—over and over using words and phrases we had mastered. We felt and acted like two-year-olds, for that's how a child learns a language: listening, repeating, learning by trial and error. But a child learns so much more quickly and easily!

In the early evenings a number of people always joined us around our outdoor fire where we cooked our meal. How could we ask their names, we wondered, when we didn't know how to say, "What is your name?"

One evening, I pointed to myself and said my name. Next I pointed at Ed and said "Dick" (the name he went by then). My name was fairly easy for the people to say, but alas! "Dick" became "Teekie."[3]

They seemed happy to know our names, but no one offered to tell us *his* name. (Later we learned that Awas are embarrassed to say their own names.) I pointed at a man and asked our now familiar question, "*Anepomo*. [What is that?]" It worked. Someone told me the man's name. But I had a strong hunch that the meaning of "*Anepomo*" didn't really extend to mean, "*Who* is that?"

A few nights later someone finally corrected us. "Don't say '*Anepomo*' about *people*. Say, '*Insebo*.'"

As we learned how to ask more questions, we began to better understand the Awa worldview.

"*Insebo*," I would ask one of the Awa women, jutting out my chin and sticking out my lower lip while pointing to a nearby man.

Oh, oh! I asked the wrong woman for *that* man's name. She turns out to be his wife. So I am scolded. "Aretta! No wife ever says her husband's name."

The woman then tells me that a wife must call her husband a nickname. Or if they have a child named, for instance, Mati, she may call him "Mati's father." Before a child is born, a wife may even call her husband the father (which also means owner) of their favorite pig!

One of the men heard me call Ed "Honey." *Now this we can pronounce*, he thought. Thereafter, to the Awas, Ed became "Ani" (pronounced A-nee, their rendition of "Honey").

If a woman reprimanded me, "You don't do good. You call your husband by his name," my defense was, "I don't call my husband by his name; you and I both call him 'Ani.' It's a custom in my country for wives to nickname their husbands after a sweet, sticky food."

The people seldom ask questions of one another—they don't need to. Living in a compact community, everyone knew not only everyone else but also everyone else's business. But this red couple had invaded their community, and not only did the people not know us, they didn't even know whether "us" were people or spirits. So they began to ask questions of us!

"Ani, is your older brother there?"

"Yes, my older brother is there," Ed would reply.

"Is your sister there?"

"No, my mother never bore a girl. Just two boys."

"Is your old mother still there?"

"Yes, she is there."

"Is your old father there?"

"No, he's not there. He died when I was a *mahbi* [a young unmarried man]."

"*Ehneh!* Red people die too?!"

"Yes, we die; we get sick; we bleed when we're cut. We're just like you."

Tipea was especially quick to ask questions. And she usually had a quick retort. But there was a time in our early language-learning days when she was speechless.

One day as I sat nursing Karen, Tipea moved close to me. She looked me in the eye. "Aretta, have you become a worthless, good-for-nothing person?"

By this time the Awas had accepted us as people rather than spirits of their ancestors. But what *kind* of people were we anyway? Who else but worthless, good-for-nothing people would "throw away [abandon]" their land and gardens, their clan, their pigs—all that made life worth living—then travel day after day over the trail, most of it a trail of water,[4] to a village not their own? And who else but worthless, good-for-nothing people would spend their days just sitting around talking rather than making gardens or tending pigs?

As I considered Tipea's question, women sat and watched as though they had appointed Tipea to ask something they all wondered about.

"No, Honey and I haven't become worthless, good-for-nothing people. We came here to tell you about our Creator Father 'Who is there [Who is alive].' If we had not come, no one would yet be able to tell you about Him."

My grasp of the Awa language wasn't adequate to tell them that this Creator Father "very much wanted each of them in His liver [loved each of them greatly]."

Tipea said nothing, but in her eyes was another question: *Could anything in life be that important?*

We cooked our food in pots rather than bamboo tubes. We had two changes of clothes, not made from bark string but made from soft lap-lap.[5] We quickly made fire by rubbing a little stick against a box. Our store-bought salt tasted so much better than their homemade variety.

In the eyes of the Awa, we were wealthy. We had not only "thrown away" our family but also, they were sure, "thrown away" huge plots of garden land and more pigs than they'd ever known one couple to own—maybe a dozen.

Is anything in life really so important that people would "throw away" family, friends, even land and pigs?

Jesus says, "The person who throws away his own thinking because he wants to follow me and tell the good news will have real life" (Mark 8:35 Awa New Testament, back-translated into English).

PRAYER

Father, grant that I shall choose what is really important in this life. The old saying is still true, "Only one life, 'twill soon be past. Only what's done for Christ will last."

TO MEDITATE ON

For whoever wants to save his life will lose it, but whoever loses his life for me and for the gospel will save it. (Mark 8:35)

Happy are those who are strong in the Lord, who want above all else to follow your steps. (Psalm 84:5 TLB)

TO ASK MYSELF

Is my desire to "save" my life? Or am I "losing" it for Jesus' sake and the gospel? Do I want above all else to follow in Jesus' steps?

---

1. A glottal stop is made by closing the glottis. In English we make a glottal stop after the first "oh" in the phrase "oh, oh!" and in a few other places. Our English alphabet does not symbolize the glottal. In Awa, it is one of the nineteen letters of the alphabet, symbolized by a *q*.
2. Questions in Awa do not have a question intonation as English has. A suffix (a marker at the end of a word) signals a question. In this case the marker is *-pomo*.
3. Awa words never begin with a *d* and never end in a *k*.
4. In 1959, we went by ship to Australia—a journey of twenty-one days. From there we flew to Papua New Guinea and landed at the port city of Lae. The next day, we caught a cargo plane to a grass airstrip seven miles from Ukarumpa center. There we unexpectedly met coworkers returning from a village—in the old World War II jeep.
5. *Lap-lap* is the Pidgin English word for cloth.

11.

Furlough or "Whirlough"?

 The transition from one country and culture to another in a few short hours is rather tremendous, isn't it? Like stepping into a new world. It's too quick really; your thoughts and impressions don't have time to catch up with your body.
—Val Bock

AT THE END OF FIVE YEARS overseas, a typical Wycliffe term for living and working overseas in the sixties, we had translated the Gospel of Mark into Awa. During those years we had studied the sound system of this formerly unwritten language and made an alphabet. We taught a few teenagers to read from primers[1] the Awas had helped us construct. Those literates we then trained and supervised as they taught others to read. About two dozen Awas could read. Two dozen more than when we first came!

From reading or hearing stories from Mark, most people in Mobuta village knew the gospel better than a typical Sunday-only-go-to-church person in the USA.

"Have you put truth to [believed in] Jesus?" we would ask.

"Oh, I pray as I walk the trail," an Awa would almost always answer.

"What do you pray?"

" '*Maniká* [Creator God], You made all this ground-ground [the world]. You sent down Your Son *Sísa*. He came down and He healed the sick. He made the lame walk. He raised the dead. He opened the eyes of the blind. People who said no to [rejected] Him stuck Him to a tree. They stuck Him there, and on that tree He died for our sins. After three days, He came alive again. He came alive, and now He's with You, our Father. Someday He will come down again to this ground.' That's what I pray."

"If you died would you go to live with Him in his Good Garden?" was our next question.

"Oh, yes…maybe."

Awa women gathered to hear stories from the Gospel of Mark

They need John's first epistle so they can know the criteria for having eternal life, we decided. So we stayed an extra six months and translated 1 John and helped more people learn to read.[2]

What will people we see on furlough think? Five and a half years and still no Christians!

That was just one of the pressures that faced us as we prepared to leave New Guinea to return to the USA. We would zigzag across the country from California (where my parents lived) to Virginia (where

Ed's mother lived). All along the way, we would visit churches and friends who prayed for us and generously gave money to keep us overseas working with the Awa people. Would our time at home turn out to be—

Furlough or "Whirlough"?

Where *is* home? Have you, like us, moved so many times that you sometimes ask yourself that question? An old song says, "This world is not my home, I'm just a-passin' through." Those words become especially meaningful after you've moved the nth time!

After five and a half years overseas, we were ready to return to the USA. We were ready for grandparents to see grandkids, and vice versa; ready to visit churches and friends and report on what God had done—and what He'd not done—with and in us those years we'd been away; ready to experience some of our own American culture and cuisine! Still we wondered about what being "home" would be like. The States were no longer really home to us and never had been home to our five-year-old Karen and three-year-old Treesa.

We wondered just what furlough held for us.

So did our daughters.

A stop in Hawaii to visit a small church that supported us with prayer broke the long trip across the ocean. That night, as we prepared to go to bed on cots set up in one of the rooms in the building where the church met, Treesa sat on my lap and sobbed, "Mommy, I want to go home!" Karen stood by with wide eyes, looking as though she might join Treesa any minute.

Whether missionaries on furlough or those who have moved from one place to another in our home country, we can react the same. We may feel like "displaced persons," wanting to "go home" but not sure just where the home we want to go to is. Karen and Treesa were already experiencing the stress of furlough!

I reached over and drew Karen toward us. "Wherever Mommy and Daddy and Karen and Treesa are together, that is home," I assured both girls. Treesa's sobs ceased. She relaxed and dropped asleep in my arms.

One mission director asked his missionaries to compare their overseas term with their furlough in this way: You are overseas on a fast merry-go-round. The music is loud, the horses go up and down as it goes around and around—and around. And it's a four-year, not a fifteen-minute, ride.

Suddenly, you're about to go on furlough. You look over and see another merry-go-round right alongside. The music is louder. The horses are bigger and more brightly colored; they go up higher and down lower. And the whole thing goes around and around in the same way—only much faster. Now, how do you jump from the first merry-go-round over to the second?

Yes, as we made that "jump," we knew our furlough could indeed turn out to be a "whirlough." *Especially for our daughters*, I thought.

But I learned that with strong parental support, the younger a child is, the less stressful a major move is. Though we crisscrossed the USA twice by car, never would a furlough be more enjoyable for Karen and Treesa. Turning never-before-seen electric lights on and off, on and off; eating peaches, pears, grapes, and oranges for the first time; playing in snow (something they'd only seen in books); making friends of cousins they'd never before met; swimming in "Gwa'ma's 'thwimming pool' ("Come see, Mommy! It's right in her bathroom!")—those were some of the things that made that furlough memorable to them.

And what made furlough memorable for Ed and me? The many churches, friends, and relatives who showed love, interest, and understanding. They helped make our time home a furlough—not a *whirlough!* After a year, we were ready to leave the USA to make our "home" in Australia for three months. There we taught linguistics at an SIL[3] school to prospective members. Then—"home" to New Guinea to once again live and work with the Awas.

A few years ago, mindful of the stress I was facing with so many moves, Treesa sent me a plaque from the Philippines. It hangs in my house wherever I abide. It reads, "Home is where the Lord sends us."

A move may be a furlough for someone living overseas. Or because of a job change for someone in his or her home country, it may be a major move from one part of the country to another (or even a minor move from one part of the city to another). But when the Lord is in the move, home is where He sends us!

PRAYER

Thank You, Father, for friends who love and understand us and who are interested in what we do. Help me—whether in my home country or overseas—to be like a thirsty sponge that first soaks up that love, understanding, and interest and then releases it to others!

TO MEDITATE ON

O Lord, you have always been our home. (Psalm 90:1 TEV)

Be joyful always; pray continually; give thanks in all circumstances, for this is God's will for you in Christ Jesus. (1 Thessalonians 5:16–18)

TO ASK MYSELF

Am I committed to follow the command "Give thanks in all circumstances" (1 Thessalonians 5:18)? Do I show interest in what others are doing? Can I joyfully agree with the statement "Home is where the Lord sends us"?

---

1. Webster defines a primer as an "elementary book for teaching [people] to read."
2. That paid off. Panuyaba and another teenager came to know Jesus Christ through reading Mark and 1 John while we were on furlough. That teenager has remained faithful to Christ to this day, and Panuyaba is now the pastor of the Mobuta village church.
3. See Appendix B.

12.

God's Radio Network

 We are often hindered from giving up our treasures to the Lord out of fear for their safety...especially...when those treasures are loved [ones]....
Everything is safe which we commit to Him, and nothing is really safe which is not so committed.
—A. W. Tozer

"WEREN'T YOU AFRAID when raising two daughters in such an isolated place?" people often ask.

Yes, at times, I was fearful. For instance, the time Treesa was a baby and had diarrhea—*bad* diarrhea (is there a *good* kind?). My precious bundle of activity was now pale and lethargic. And the nearest clinic was two long, hard days' hike away.

"I feel we ought to stop the medicine and just trust God to heal her," Ed said.

"But surely the medicine will soon begin to have an effect," I countered. But it didn't.

That evening as I stood by her pole crib after giving her another dose of medicine, I cried out, "Lord, please, heal my baby!"

I heard a soft whisper in my spirit. "I will if you stop the medicine."

Treesa began to get better immediately as I obeyed the Holy Spirit's prompting.

Raising our daughters where there was no medical help taught me that the Great Physician is always near. I also learned that the Lord has a network of His children "out there" and He can contact them anytime He wants to use them in my life by use of—

God's Radio Network

By her screams I knew our six-year-old Karen was at least alive and conscious. We dashed out of the house to find her. She had been swinging on the clothesline when the heavy wooden post, rotted from frequent tropical rains, had fallen and hit her on the head. Her screaming subsided as she responded to our comfort. "I want to go to my bed," she sobbed. "I want to go to my bed and sleep."

Sleep! I screamed inwardly. *What if she goes to sleep and never wakes up?*

It was 1966, and we were in Mobuta village, isolated from medical help. A twelve- to fourteen-hour trek over rugged mountain ridges and across rushing streams would bring us to the nearest medical post. At that time, our group in PNG had no helicopters, only Cessnas. And the mountainous terrain in Awaland did not lend itself to building an airstrip. But way out there in our village home, we did have a *Pioneer*! JAARS* man Jim Baptista specially designed the *Pioneer*, a lightweight two-way radio, for translators like us living in remote areas. How thankful we were for that radio. It gave my mother-heart some feeling of security.

"If only I could talk to someone on the radio!" I lamented, then continued, more to myself than to Ed, "If only I could talk to Marj. She's a nurse, and she could tell us what to do."

Marj and Ernie, fellow translators, lived in another remote part of New Guinea. Each morning they "checked in" with our main center on their two-way radio, as we and other coworkers also routinely did on our radios. Often at that 7 a.m. check-in, conversations were scheduled for later in the day. But that day the next scheduled contact wasn't until four o'clock—four long hours away!

"By four o'clock Karen could...." I pushed away the icy fear, refusing to let it form itself into words in my mind. I had to try something! So despite my ever practical husband's reminder that "no one will be on the radio at 12 noon," I switched on the transmitter of the *Pioneer*.

"This is Quebec Sierra," I began, giving our call-sign as radio protocol dictated. "This is Quebec Sierra calling...." I hesitated. Who was I calling anyway? I knew all too well that Ed was right. With sinking heart, as I sat there holding the microphone, I admitted to myself that, indeed, no one would be on the radio at this hour.

Nevertheless, "This is Quebec Sierra calling ANYBODY," I blurted out. "Is ANYBODY on the air?"

Almost immediately a voice responded. Marj!

As I answered her questions, she calmly assured me that Karen was showing no real danger signs. Even so, she suggested that we keep Karen awake for the next hour or so and watch her responses.

I turned from the radio, with my "what-if" fears at rest, and hurried back to a still sobbing Karen.

"How would you like Mommy to read *Charlotte's Web* to you?" I asked, not really giving her a choice.

Once again Charlotte spun her magic gossamer, captivating Karen's attention and causing Karen to respond with her usual enthusiasm to her favorite book.

By nightfall our daughter was once again the same energetic six-year-old she'd been. The only tangible reminders of the incident were a wiser Karen with a large goose egg on her head and a new clothesline post for me. Little sister Treesa had admonished her big sister, "Don't do dat ag'in, Ka-wen," and Ed had teamed up with one of the village men to fix the clothesline, his way of keeping his fears in rein.

A couple of months later, when back at our main center for Conference, I asked Marj why she had come on the radio that day.

"I was in my kitchen fixing lunch," she said, "and the Holy Spirit seemed to whisper to me, 'Turn on the radio.' So I did."

Tears came to my eyes. Our heavenly Father had known all along that Karen would be all right, but He understood the concerns and fears of Karen's mother. It was He who had given Jim the idea for and technical expertise to assemble the *Pioneer*. And that day, so that my mind would be at peace, He involved another of His children in our fearful drama, gently speaking to a heart tuned to hear His voice. How caring is our God!

PRAYER

Father, tune my heart to hear Your voice frequency so that I become Your channel of blessing to others!

TO MEDITATE ON

Before they call I will answer; while they are still speaking I will hear. (Isaiah 65:24)

Do not be afraid....For I am with you, and no one is going to attack and harm you, because I have many people in this city [state, country, world]. (Acts 18:9–10)

TO ASK MYSELF

Am I holding back from going somewhere God is directing because I'm fearful for my own safety or the safety of my children? Knowing that life is a gift from God and that He loves me and my loved ones more than I ever could, can I trust Him to take care of me—and them—anywhere He sends me?

---

* See Appendix F.

13.

A Bride for Panuyaba

 He knows, He loves, He cares,
Nothing this faith can dim.
He only gives the best to those
Who leave the choice to Him.
—Anonymous

IN 1959, PANUYABA, ALONG with several of his peers, had just been made a *mahbi*. The village elders had woven long bark string into his black, kinky hair. On top of that long wig, Panuyaba wore a half-crown of cassowary feathers flanked with a headband of small, white seashells.[1] The small piece of cane worn in his pierced nose septum would be replaced periodically by larger pieces of cane to enlarge the hole.

One day an Awa boy is just that: a *boy* living with his mother, fed and cared for by her; the next, after an initiation ceremony, he's a *mahbi*. A *mahbi* must leave the warmth and security of his mother's small dwelling to live with other initiates in a large "*mahbi* house," where he's on his own!

All of this is in preparation for an initiation in another few years that each *mahbi* must go through. At this second initiation ceremony, that enlarged hole in the septum is filled with large pig tusks. The whole village becomes involved preparing for this important initiation.

It was time for Panuyaba and his peers to undergo that initiation. Panuyaba's fathers[2] stayed up late, sitting around a smoldering fire, smoking bamboo pipes, pondering and deliberating. It was on their shoulders that the responsibility fell for choosing—

A Bride for Panuyaba

It was marrying time in the valley—an occasion wherein several young men and women would undergo the rite of a marriage ceremony.

Fathers of the grooms had chosen which pig they would slaughter for their new in-laws on this festive occasion.

The bodies of the grooms glistened with rancid-smelling pig fat. Long strands of bark string were twined into the grooms' kinky locks. Each face was a work of art painted in red ocher and black soot. Around the young men's necks hung large, white cowrie shells. Heads topped with a half-crown of black cassowary feathers were held high, showing off the "wedding rings": large, ivory-colored pig tusks worn in the septa of the men's noses. Ankles sported intricately woven bands that had stolen hours of gardening time from the women. The men's costumes were completed by bark skirts decorated with paints extracted from tree nuts. As the men strutted about, their skirts made a pleasant swishing sound.

Brides, too, were attired in wedding regalia, though the beauty of a bride's costume in no way matched that of her elegant groom's. These young women had been chosen by the grooms' fathers as they bargained with the fathers of the brides months, or even years, in advance. Most of the young men were delighted with their fathers' choices.

Most. But not Panuyaba. From the time he was a small boy running over the hills, catching grasshoppers, and digging beetles to roast over the evening fire, he had set his eye on Sehuraqmara. As she grew to womanhood, she impressed him with her quickness; with her stamina to dig up large garden plots; with her ability to spend the day gardening, then climb the steep mountain trails carrying a heavy bag of sweet potatoes slung by a strap over her forehead. He wanted Sehuraqmara! No other young woman in the village was half as desirable; no other young woman worked half as hard.

But Panuyaba's fathers had decreed, "You will marry Wehria, Sehuraqmara's older sister!"

Wehria? None of the young men wanted her. She was as different from her sister as the white cockatoo was from the glistening blue-black singing starling. As the young men turned their sweet potatoes over the fires in the evening, they talked. All knew that Wehria was lazy. But custom dictated that older sisters marry first.

Panuyaba did not usually defy his fathers' orders, but this time, he insisted, "I will marry *Sehuraqmara.*"

Still the word from his fathers was "Wehria!" Yesterday they had proposed a compromise. "All right, marry Sehuraqmara. But you must also take Wehria."

When Panuyaba was about fourteen years old, two outsiders had come to live in his village. His people wondered, *Why have these red ones come? Are they the spirits of our ancestors?*

As they watched and wondered, the couple began to learn their language. One day they knew enough to ask the elders, "Who made these mountains, rocks and trees, the moon and stars?"

"Maniká," they replied. *How dense these red ones are. Why, even a child knows that!*

"Tell us about Him," the couple responded.

"We don't know anything about Him. Just that He made everything, then He left. He's up there. Sometimes He roars and shoots down bolts of fire. If He's really angry, He shakes the earth."

This red couple seemed to know a lot about *Maniká. Maniká* "wanted them in His liver [loved them]." He sent His Son—*Sísa Karáhé*—down to earth. *Sísa* healed the sick, opened the eyes of the blind, made the deaf hear, even raised the dead. He taught people about *Maniká*, His Father, and claimed that He and *Maniká* were one. "*Sísa* loved you so much that He died in your place for all your 'goofing up,'" they told Panuyaba and his people.

With the help of village men, the red couple began to write a book. *Manikáne O Ehwehne* [God's New Talk], they called the book. The red woman taught Panuyaba and a few other young men to read their own language. Panuyaba read and put truth to [believed] the talk in the book. Because of that, his fathers' compromise was not acceptable. "Sísa lives in my liver. Therefore I cannot take two wives."

"You are our child; you are not the child of those red ones. You must follow our talk, not their talk," his fathers answered, their faces tight with anger.

"I am not following *their* talk. I'm carrying on my shoulders [obeying] *Maniká*'s talk. The Book says, 'Each man should take his own wife.' It does not say 'wives.'"

Now it was the day before the ceremony. Exhausted from arguing, Panuyaba sat under a tree in the forest. The final word, "You must also take Wehria," rang in his ears; it rang louder than the many buzzing insects swarming around his head.

"O *Maniká*, my Father, I am too small to change my fathers' thinking. But You are bigger than all the big men in my village, and You can change their thinking," Panuyaba prayed. Then he went down to his house and slept peacefully through the cold highlands night.

"Panuyaba-o-o-o-o!" His fathers' call awoke him the next morning.

Panuyaba stood before the elders knowing his words were on *Maniká*'s ear [God had heard his prayer]. His liver was at rest.

"Our son," his oldest father began, "we sat by the fire and talked late into the night. We have changed our thinking. You may take only Sehuraqmara."

Panuyaba could not help almost breaking the taboo of a groom never smiling on his wedding day. But he quickly recovered. Dropping his eyes, he simply said, "My fathers, you do well." Then he turned and walked away. And although no smile broke through the pig grease and soot, his liver danced and cried out, "O *Maniká*, *Sísa Karáhé*, You truly are the Big One!"

POSTSCRIPT: The people in this fictionalized account of true happenings are real people. Today the Awas have the Book (the New Testament) in their own language. Panuyaba is the pastor of the church in his village. He and Sehuraqmara share with their people, as well as people from other villages, the "Sweet Potato of Life" (the Awa equivalent of the Bread of Life).

PRAYER

Father, our hearts echo Panuyaba's prayer: You truly are the Big One, the Almighty God. We worship You.

TO MEDITATE ON

This is what the LORD says: "...I will come to you and fulfill my gracious promise.... For I know the plans I have for you," declares the LORD, "plans to prosper you and not to harm you, plans to give you hope and a future." (Jeremiah 29:10–11)

TO ASK MYSELF

Do I really believe that if I leave the choice regarding my future to Him, He will give me His best?

---

1. Along trade routes, small, white cowrie shells, as well as larger ones, found their way up into the highlands. The Awas did not know they were seashells, but they highly valued them, using them as money. They displayed this wealth by wearing cowrie shell necklaces and headbands.
2. In Awa culture, uncles are called "fathers" and collectively function as such when a person's birth father is dead.

14.

The Dark Packet's Power

Choose today whom you will serve. Would you prefer the gods your ancestors served…? But as for me and my family, we will serve the LORD.
—Joshua 24:15 NLT

SEHURAQMARA—A SMALL, shy child she was, just one of the many *méra-mehra* of Mobuta village. She must have been nine or ten years old in 1959. At the time, we thought she was no more than six.

The bags of sweet potatoes this wiry little girl carried up from her mother's riverside garden were almost as heavy as she was. Ah, yes, Sehuraqmara would grow up to be a "bent-backed woman." She would turn over large plots of ground with her digging stick, or with a store-bought spade if she was lucky enough to own one. In that ground she would plant and harvest sweet potatoes for her family. No one would ever be able to slander her by calling her a "straight-backed [lazy]" person!

Over the years as we watched this child-in-the-faith of ours following Jesus, we learned what the apostle John meant when he said, "I have no greater joy than to hear that my children are walking in the truth" (3 John 4).

A fictionalized account from Sehuraqmara's point of view of the drama of the previous chapter reveals—

The Dark Packet's Power

Sehuraqmara sat in the smoke-filled house, head bowed. She stared into the glowing coals. Korani sat beside her and with long, bamboo tongs turned the sweet potatoes roasting in the hot ashes.

"Awake, Sleepy One!" Korani spoke loudly as she poked Sehuraqmara with the tongs. Then handing the tool to her daughter, she ordered, "Turn that sweet potato near you."

Mother and daughter, laden with heavy loads of sweet potato and firewood, had climbed the 2,000-foot incline from their riverside garden. After stashing most of the wood under the eaves, they had quickly escaped the chill of the mountain air. Inside their small thatch dwelling, they scurried about in a race against nightfall. Korani barricaded the narrow entrance with lengths of bamboo to shut out not only the drifting fog but also the evil *wahnsa** who roam about under cover of darkness seeking to attack and cause sickness. Soon a blazing fire devoured the darkness.

The warmth usually caused Sehuraqmara to doze long before she retired to her woven bamboo mat. But not tonight. *She thinks I'm sleepy. After this morning how could I sleep? Where is Panuyaba right now? Is he cold?* Sehuraqmara's thoughts darted about like an orphaned piglet thrashing through forest underbrush to dodge the hunters' arrows.

The moon is new. So dark out there! Sehuraqmara shuddered as she heard an eerie sound. The wind? Or her dead father's *wahnsa* whistling? She reached into her bag and closed her hand around a small packet wrapped in a banana leaf.

Is Panuyaba really no longer afraid of the spirits? He has put truth to Sísa—this One the red couple are writing a book about? Will Panuyaba bow to the pressure of the elders and take Wehria as his wife?

A jab with the tongs poked into her crowded thoughts. "Here! Lest your dry liver die of hunger, eat this! Then curl up on your mat and go to sleep!" Korani ordered, unaware that hunger was not the cause of Sehuraqmara's "dry liver."

Sehuraqmara took the sweet potato her mother held out to her. *Does Panuyaba have sweet potato tonight?* she wondered as she blew ashes from the hot tuber. *He says* Sísa *is "the Sweet Potato of Life." What does he mean?*

The aroma of the steaming sweet potato collided with her racing thoughts. It transported her back to earlier in the day to remind her that she hadn't eaten since midmorning.

Her liver had swelled with joy this morning when Panuyaba had declared to the elders, "I do not want to marry Wehria. I will marry Sehuraqmara."

It was then she had taken a cold sweet potato from her bag and eaten it, her eyes fastened on the elders gathered in a tight circle. Panuyaba had sat near them. *He knows that my liver is one with his.* Sehuraqmara had not yet "put truth to" Panuyaba's God, *Sísa,* so she had quickly added, *at least about marrying him.*

The circle had broken and Panuyaba's oldest uncle had stepped forward. "All right. You may marry Sehuraqmara," he had announced.

But then Uncle had continued, and Sehuraqmara's joy had been severed. Severed as quickly as those new steel knives slash the forest vines used in house building. "You may marry Sehuraqmara, but you must also take her older sister. It is not fitting that the younger marry first. You must take Wehria also."

Panuyaba had stood to his feet. *So regal in his cassowary headdress! Like a god from the elders' fireside stories,* Sehuraqmara had mused. *What will he tell them? I could never be happy as a second wife.*

Panuyaba's words had lightened her heavy liver. "If I had not put truth to *Sísa,* I would take both. But now I cannot take two wives."

His boldness had infuriated the elders. "You are our child, not the child of that red man. Do not follow his talk; do what we say!"

"I am not following his talk. I am doing what the Book says. The Book says each man is to have his own *wife*; it does not say *wives*."

Korani poked the fire, and Sehuraqmara's thoughts returned to the present. She opened her string bag and reached in and touched the banana-leaf-wrapped packet. A year ago she had yanked hair from her dying father's head and wrapped it in a banana leaf. After his death, day and night she wore the amulet around her neck, until one day.

"Throw it away and put truth to *Sísa*. *Sísa* is stronger than your father's *wahnsa*. He will protect you," Panuyaba had encouraged her.

Throw it away and risk the wrath of my dead father? With trembling hands she had removed the amulet from her neck. It had found its way into her string bag. Since that day the bag had gone with her wherever she went—to her gardens, to the spring for water, to village meetings.

Sehuraqmara now lay on her bamboo bed. *"Sleepy One" she called me. Now she is the one curled up snoring. And I am like a forest spirit-dog {owl}perched on a limb watching over Panuyaba there on his cold bed. Or is* Sísa *watching over him?*

Suddenly she sat up and reached for her bag. She took out the amulet. *Panuyaba says* Sísa *is stronger than the spirits. Is He really strong enough to protect me from my father's* wahnsa?

Korani snorted and turned on her mat. Sehuraqmara held her breath and sat very still. Once Korani's snoring returned to a rhythmic pattern, she crawled to the fire pit. She raked deep into the ashes and unearthed a glowing coal. Placing the coal on a bundle of twigs, she softly blew on it. Soon a dancing flame rewarded her efforts. Quickly, before her crowded thoughts could choke her intention, she placed the amulet on the flame. The flame jumped up and hungrily curled itself around the dry banana leaves. Just as quickly, it dimmed as though bowing to the darkness of the amulet. The stench of searing hair caused Korani once again to snort and turn.

What have I done? What will Korani say? What will my father's spirit do? Sehuraqmara's thoughts tumbled one over another. Then Panuyaba's words jumped up, as that flame had. But unlike the flame, they did not dim. Rather, they blazed into light and wrapped her with warmth and comfort. "He will protect you. He will protect you. He will protect...."

"Sleepy One, awake! It's morning." Korani laughed and handed her a sweet potato, one she had roasted hours earlier. "The elders have gathered."

Sehuraqmara hurriedly crawled out of the dark hut into the sunshine. *Light. Bright like the light that entered my liver last night. Was that Sísa?*

Once again Panuyaba stood before the elders in his bridegroom finery. And once again Uncle spoke for the elders. "We sat by the fire late into the night and talked. We have decided you may marry Sehuraqmara only."

"My fathers, as I lay all night in the forest under the large *entua* tree, I told *Sísa,* 'I am not strong enough to change the thinking of my fathers. Only You are strong enough to do that.' Now I have heard you speak well." He walked away, ready for the groom initiation that would pledge him to Sehuraqmara.

"Yes, *Sísa is* stronger than the spirits. The elders' thinking—how hard it is! Hard as the sun-baked ground. Yet He has changed their thinking. Now I know He is strong enough to protect me. O *Sísa,* I put truth to You," Sehuraqmara whispered, and her liver danced with joy.

The Panuyaba family and their piglets.

PRAYER

Thank You, Father God, that we do not have to depend on anything we have or do for protection from the evil one. Thank You that by Your power You protect us when we trust You above all else.

TO MEDITATE ON

But you belong to God, my dear children. You have already won your fight with these false prophets, because the Spirit who lives in you is greater than the spirit who lives in the world. (1 John 4:4 NLT)

But you are a chosen people, a royal priesthood, a holy nation, a people belonging to God, that you may declare the praises of him who called you out of darkness into his wonderful light. (1 Peter 2:9)

TO ASK MYSELF

Do I truly believe in my heart that I have already won the fight? That I am chosen, that I belong to God? Am I walking in that wonderful light into which He has called me?

---

* The Awa believed that when a man died, he became a *wahnsa*. A *wahnsa* was invisible and had the power to beat people, causing them to become sick. The wife and children of the dead man were especially susceptible.

15.

Stepping on My Toes

 With small children in a home, it should be easy to "count your blessings"—if the children would only sit still and let you count!
—Bill Keane

MÉRA-MEHRA (PRONOUNCED MAYDA-MAD-DA) is the Awa word for children. Lots of children! The repetitive syllables reflect that when lots of Awa kids get together they do this, do that; then they do this and do that again. Yes, Awa children are like children everywhere— they have a hard time sitting still.

On a rainy day, the *méra-mehra* with their muddy feet crowded into our bamboo and thatch house and sat on the woven bamboo floor. Some looked at *National Geographic* magazines; others played with toys from the toy bag. All liked to peruse, for the umpteenth time, albums of photos from long ago and a few recent ones with pictures of themselves in them. They would sing Awa church songs for us. What a contrast with the early days! The only songs the children knew then were those invoking the spirits.

When my tolerance for being watched wasn't at frustration level, I allowed them to simply sit and stare at me. What could be more exciting than watching a red-skinned woman, especially if she's cooking *páréti*? She mixes white stuff [flour] with something called "with-the-potential-to-make-it-swell stuff [yeast]." She adds a few tablespoons of other white stuff [powdered milk]. Then a couple of teaspoons of *sóreq*. Sometimes she sprinkles a bit of *sóreq*—as the Awas call store-bought salt—in the palm of each child's hand. She is rewarded by a measure of quietness for the next ten minutes or so as the children occupy themselves by taking dainty licks of the wonderful stuff.

Méra-mehra with bottles ready to go for drinking water from the local spring.

From a big barrel, the red woman dips water and pours it into the dry mixture. Finally she puts this in metal pans, not bamboo tubes! She cooks it, not over an open fire but in a box [oven] next to where the wood is burning.

Yes, I'm the "red" woman who made yeast bread in the village. The crowd of *méra-mehra* with dirty feet transports me back to a time long ago. I remember a little boy whose feet were not only dirty but also scaly. We once took him to Ukarumpa in the helicopter so the clinic doctor could diagnose and advise treatment. "You can relieve his skin problem some by treatment," I was told (and I did) "but it's a fatal disease."*

Although Sokari's life was short, he taught me something about how I should react to my heavenly Father. You see, Sokari had a habit of—

Stepping on My Toes

A sad little boy he was, always clothed in nothing more than sunshine and a scowl. Cross-eyed, knock-kneed, scaly-skinned, dirty—that was six-year-old Sokari. He didn't come around our house much. When he did, he watched us from a distance interact with other Awa kids.

One day Sokari teamed up with Inauga, a precocious young lady about the same age as he. They took bananas from our outside food-storage table. How it delighted the other kids to tattle on Sokari and Inauga. You would have thought they were identifying confirmed bank robbers!

How would I handle this? *I can't let them think stealing is okay, despite the fact that a couple of bananas is no big deal*, I reasoned.

"Tell them both to come," I instructed one of the bigger boys. They came: Inauga, smiling, with an "I know you, Aretta-Old-Woman; your bark is worse than your bite" attitude; Sokari with an "I don't know you and I'm terrified!" attitude.

First, I lectured the two budding young bank robbers. I then lifted Inauga's tiny bark skirt and lightly swatted her bare bottom. The result—a smirk that said, "Is that all? Those bananas were worth those three swats!"

Then Sokari. No G-string to lift. *Can I bring myself to hit this scaly little bottom—even lightly?* I wondered. *But he needs to know that stealing food is a "not-done-thing."* After I delivered his three swats, he stood in silence. Huge tears channeled their way around the scales on his cheeks, carrying rivulets of mud with them. I stifled the urge to take this sad little child in my arms and comfort him.

The next day as I stood talking to a group of people, I felt a small body press close to my leg. Not unusual. Awa kids often did that. It was their way of letting me know they were there, their way of saying,

"I like you." Then a foot was placed on my foot. I looked down. Crossed eyes looked up at me, and a dirty, scaly-skinned face emitted a shy smile. I smiled back, then reached down and took his hand.

From that day onward, I could expect that if Sokari was around me, he would have a small, horny foot on top of my foot. He would stand and hold my hand as he pressed his bare body close to my leg.

May I be like Sokari! May I accept the discipline of the One who loves me, who wants only the best for me. Then pressing close to Him, let me look up into His face. He'll smile back and reach down and take my hand.

PRAYER

Lord, thank You that You cared when there was nothing beautiful in me to cause You to love me. I want to "step on Your toes," to come close to You. I want to feel You reach down and take my hand.

TO MEDITATE ON

Come near to God and he will come near to you. (James 4:8)

Yet I am always with you; you hold me by my right hand. (Psalm 73:23)

I, the LORD, have called you in righteousness; I will take hold of your hand. I will keep you.... (Isaiah 42:6)

TO ASK MYSELF

When I do wrong, do I accept God's discipline, repent, and then press close to Him? Or do I let my sin keep me from Him?

---

* Scleroderma, a chronic disease in which the skin becomes hard and rigid, is "a sometimes fatal skin disease," according to the February 1996 *Science News*, Vol. 149, No. 6 page 85. Scleroderma was probably the skin disease Sokari had.

16.

A Head Lifted High

> If [God] has work for me to do I cannot die.
> —Henry Martyn

SO MANY THINGS TO FEAR! Before the Awas heard the good news "Fear not!" from the Book in their language, they lived in constant fear.

From the time an Awa child first began to walk, his elders cautioned him to never walk anywhere alone. "*Wahnsa sabiehboq...*" they told the child. That phrase, "Lest the spirits..." carried the implied message that anytime the spirits found him alone, they would jump on him and beat his bones into pulp. The child would then become sick and die.

When out in the garden with his mother, a child would also hear, "*Wehe sabiehboq...* [Lest the death adder...]." As its name implies, if this short, brown snake bites a child, the child dies.

Another fear the Awa child—as well as the mother of an Awa child—daily lived with was pay-back killing![1] The child might awaken one morning to hear that his father had been brutally slain.

When Awas came to know God, they experienced His power to deliver. They saw—

A Head Lifted High

After the chilly highland night, the sun felt warm on Matiro's broad back. It was good to be working in his sweet potato garden. He recalled when he was a little boy and the weather had turned very cold. The next morning a white "stuff" had appeared all over the ground, covering his father's sweet potato vines. The tropical sun had soon melted that "stuff," leaving the vines brown and wilted. Matiro recalled lying on his sleeping mat at night, snuggled close to his mother for comfort. Hunger had "chewed holes in his insides," like the rats chewed holes in his mother's bark-string bag when she forgot to stuff it into a bamboo tube container.

That cold, white stuff had appeared in their garden only twice in his lifetime. How glad he was that it had not come since he had become a man and responsible for his old mother and a young, growing family. He was thankful for a good crop this year. It would feed him and his family well.

Someone coughed, interrupting his thoughts. He turned. A band of men had come stealthily, so he had not heard them approach. But now Matiro[2] faced them as they stood armed with bows and arrows. Some held fighting clubs. Steel axes glinted in the sun as they dangled from the men's belts. The men walked toward Matiro, their faces harder than the stones he dug up and threw out of his garden.

Slowly the men encircled Matiro, who felt that his feet were rooted in his garden, rooted firmer than the sweet potato vines. The men's hot hatred seared into his chest and back, burning him more than the midday tropical sun. It penetrated into his very soul.

These men were not *his* enemies; rather, they were his father's enemies. But as was the custom of his people, enmity passed down from one generation to the next. Matiro's only crime—he was the son of his father! He did not hate these men; they hated him simply because he had been born to his father.

Matiro thought of his childhood, of the days of freedom, running over the hills, shooting lizards, and catching grasshoppers to roast over the evening fire. The memory of those fires and his mother's warm body made him feel safe for a moment. Then he thought of his father, a renowned warrior. His father, like these men, had done pay-back killings; he had killed young men because of the crimes of *their* fathers.

But that was before the pale red man came. He had come saying he would write a book in the language of Matiro's people, the language that spoke so clearly to Matiro's liver. It was a book, the red man said, about a Creator God who loved them. This God did not expect them to give things to Him. No, *He* gave to *them*. He had even given His one and only Son—*Sísa* was His name—as a sacrifice to die for Matiro's sins.

Matiro understood this, for he, the son of his father, was about to be sacrificed. But, oh, how different would be his death. It would not bring life, peace, and joy to people as the death of Jesus had. It would only further harden the old hatred so carefully preserved by his people. No, it would not bring life; it would bring more hatred, more revenge, more pay-back killings. And for that he felt sad. Yet he also felt peace deep down in his liver. He did not want to die, but if God wanted him to go, he was ready to meet this God he had come to know, to love, and to trust. He wanted to live, to continue helping the red man write the book. "I cannot write the book alone; I need your help," the red man told Matiro again and again.

Matiro stood looking into the cold, hard eyes of his father's enemies. In the old days, a man would never be alone in his garden, for he feared the spirits as much as or more than traditional enemies. But because Matiro had asked Jesus to live in his liver, he knew that the one Great Spirit was more powerful than the spirits he had been taught to fear as a child. He no longer feared them. How strange, he thought, that he didn't even feel afraid of these men with their dark, evil faces.

He could try to defend himself with his spade. But that would only make them angrier. Words from the Book came to his mind. "Do not resist...." *How did the rest of it go?* He could not remember. That was why he was helping to write the Book in his language.

Matiro dropped to his knees and bowed his head. He could at least meet Jesus in this position. Jesus had bowed His head on the cross for him.

"O Big One, somewhere in Your Book it says that when people persecute me, You bless me. Thank You for blessing me now. Last week the red man and I worked on a part of Your Book that tells us to bless the people who persecute us. So I bless my father's enemies. My Father, You are able to put Your big *tenke* [wooden shield] in front of me. Or You can let these men kill me. I would like to live. I want to hear my baby daughter laugh again. I want to see her reach her arms out to me when I come home from checking my traps in the forest. I want to walk the path holding my son's hand again. I want to eat sweet potato with my wife again.

"Once we have finished writing the Book, I want to go to Bible school. There I will study the Book and learn how to teach it to my people. I want them to know You so these pay-back killings won't keep happening."

Matiro paused. A groan from deep within escaped from his mouth. "But don't do what I want, my Big Father. Do what You want."

Matiro prayed on and on, lost in his praying as much as he had been lost in his thinking before the men came. Finally, prayed out, he opened his eyes.

Had it been a horrible vision, those men standing there with their bows and arrows, clubs, and axes? Had Matiro really seen them? He arose and walked around the circle where the men had stood—or was it where he *thought* they had stood? No, there were their footprints. They *had* been here. He had not hallucinated as he used to after he chewed the black mushroom to put him in contact with the spirits.

Once again Matiro dropped to his knees. "O Father, it is as though You raised me from the dead!"

Matiro's enemies were nowhere in sight. Somehow, the One who had truly been raised from the dead had caused these enemies to leave.

This time Matiro did not bow his head. He raised it heavenward and lifted his hands in praise to the God who died with bowed head, then arose victorious over His enemies with head lifted high!

PRAYER

Lord Jesus, You prayed, "Father, if you are willing, take this cup from me; yet not my will, but yours be done" (Luke 22:41). I want to be like You! Whatever comes my way, may I say as Matiro said, "Don't do what I want, my Big Father. Do what You want."

TO MEDITATE ON

For Jehovah is our light and our Protector. He gives us grace and glory. No good thing will he withhold *from those who walk along his paths*. O Lord of the armies of heaven, blessed are those who trust in you. (Psalm 84:11–12 TLB, emphasis mine)

He is for me! How can I be afraid? What can mere man do to me? (Psalm 118:6 TLB)

TO ASK MYSELF

In times of trial do I say, as Matiro did, "Don't do what I want, my Big Father. Do what You want"? Am I walking along His paths? If so, I am a candidate for those "good things" He wants to give me!

---

1. Refer to the footnote in Chapter 4 on pay-back.
2. Though this account is fictionalized, the incident is a real happening.

17.

TVitis

 It came as a hard lesson for me to learn, but I have discovered that God can bless people I disagree with…people who may have different ideas and interpretations, or different methods, from my own.
—Warren Wiersbe

"KAREN! TREESA! YOU WERE reading instead of getting ready for school this morning. For a week, you both are banned from reading books—except ones I choose!"

Whenever I told friends in our home country of this method of discipline, they would exclaim, "If only we could have the problem of our children reading too much!"

Reading was very important to Karen and Treesa. Not only did we have no indoor plumbing or electric lights our first five and a half years in Papua New Guinea, but also we owned no TV during all our daughters' growing-up years. I learned that was just *one* of the many advantages of living overseas.

Regrettably, however, living overseas with no TV did not automatically ensure we were free from—

TVitis

I remember the day it dawned on our younger daughter Treesa that her mother just might have existed before the days of TV.

"Mommy, do you remember the days when there was no TV?"

"I sure do, Treesa!"

"Not even black and white TV, Mommy?"

"Not even black and white TV. No TV. Zilch!"

That last word I added to communicate that although my ten-year-old daughter obviously considered her mother an anomaly from the distant past, I knew and could use modern slang. I might as well have saved the strain on my vocal cords. Treesa's look of awe told me she felt as though she were standing before ancient history reenacted in live, color TV.

Years later, Karen, in her first year of college, was introduced to the big world of intriguing TV and *radio* soap operas, accompanied by endless commercials. On one campus visit, I was greeted with the revealing news, "Mom, did you know that they even have soap operas on radio these days?"

Memories of rushing home from school to hear "Ma Perkins" on the radio caused me to smile. I remember when the time it came on was changed so we could no longer get home in time to hear the show. First thing home, over a cookie and a glass of milk in a warm kitchen, Mom would relate to my sister and me the latest happenings with dear old Ma!

Yes, *I* knew radio was the harbinger of soap operas. But as far as Karen was concerned, soap operas were born and bred on television.

Our daughters' reactions were natural for their ages and background. They remind me of how often we tend to have TVitis (tunnel-vision-itis). That is, we see and hear things only from our point of view, oblivious to the concerns and opinions of others.

In one of his books, Robert Fulghum said that "most of what we see other people do, we don't know *why* they do it." He concluded that in most cases it's hard to judge without a lot more information. But "we go ahead and judge anyway," he said.* God's Word enjoins each of us to "judge not, lest you be judged by the same judgment" (Matthew 7:1).

PRAYER

O Lord, purge from me from the thinking that judges others with an attitude that communicates, "Unless you see and do as I see and do, you're wrong!"

TO MEDITATE ON

Each of you should look not only to your own interests, but also to the interests of others. (Philippians 2:4)

Do not judge, or you too will be judged. For in the same way you judge others, you will be judged.... (Matthew 7:1–2)

TO ASK MYSELF

In what areas am I having "eye problems"?

---

* Robert Fulghum, *It Was On Fire When I Lay Down on It*, New York: Ivy Books.

18.

The Leaf Has Fallen

 Jesus said, "…haven't you read in God's Word, 'From the mouths of children and babies I'll furnish a place of praise'?"
—Matthew 21:16 *The Message*

BOTH KAREN AND TREESA have fond memories of growing up in Papua New Guinea. We attribute that in no small part to those support workers who served at Ukarumpa as children's home parents. Each home housed twelve children and two parents.

"Uncle" Graham and "Aunt" Muriel Collier were favorites of the girls. This Australian couple later felt God call them to do village work, encouraging people to learn to read by training literacy supervisors and teachers. Literacy is a vital part of Bible translation, for without readers, the translated Scripture remains a closed book.

Children's home parents "Uncle" David and "Aunt" Daphne Lithgow, also "Aussies," were another favorite of the girls. David* played the guitar and taught the children to sing Australian outback songs! David, a medical doctor, and Daphne, a bacteriologist and an accomplished pianist, first served with another mission. "We were just treating bodies; there was no time for the spiritual," they reported.

After resigning from that mission, David and Daphne received training in linguistics and Bible translation and joined Wycliffe as translators. Since they had four children of their own, one year they put their translation work on hold and served as children's home parents. Even so, they finished three New Testament translations and were about to complete the fourth when God called David to his heavenly home.

Dedicated schoolteachers also had vital input into our daughters' lives. Ger Reesink, a translator who filled in as a high school teacher one year, was from the Netherlands. Karen came home one day and reported in all sincerity, "Mr. Reesink once saved Holland from a flood. He stood all day with his finger in a dike!"

Karen was not the only one to learn late in life about the famous *American* fable of the little Dutch boy who saved his country from a flood. Ger had never heard the story until he and his family came to PNG. As our group became more established in PNG, more and more couples, especially retired couples, came specifically to be children's home parents and teachers. That meant translators didn't have to fill this need.

Mr. Harder (teachers were not Uncle-ed and Auntie-ed) was often quoted by our girls as an authority on any given subject. He and Alice were Canadians, and both taught at our group grade school for many years, molding the lives of our daughters and many other MKs.

Denise Potts, a teacher from England, came as an STA. Although STA stands for short-term assistant, we often say it really means sure to apply. And that is just what Miss Potts did. She became a member and joined Dottie James, a single woman translator, to work in literacy.

Karen and Treesa had the opportunity to take piano lessons. In high school, both even gave lessons to beginners, thus earning spending money. Sports, art and science fairs, musicals and dramas, evangelistic outreaches, campouts—all these were a part of our daughters' experience, plus lots of the good old solid three Rs.

With such a colorful array of teachers from so many different cultural backgrounds, it's no wonder our children received an excellent education, despite their not knowing all the great American myths.

A fiction-based-on-fact article that Treesa wrote for an advanced placement high school English class showed us not only that her talent for writing blossomed under these devoted teachers but also that she longed to see Awa people come to know Jesus. Her story she called—

The Leaf Has Fallen

He was a wizened old man, toothless and ancient. As young as I was, whenever I saw him, I had a vague feeling that he resembled a dried and wrinkled prune. He clung to life, the last leaf on the tree with the snow swirling down. His hair, snow white and fluffy, was a great contrast to his black leathery skin and was the only softness he had. The rest of him was hard; just gaunt bones with skin stretched over his slight skeleton, dried but with dips and wrinkles.

So I saw him when I came around the beehive house. The *kunai* grass thatch that was left on the house was thick with soot. The bamboo walls sagged. Later when I was older, it dawned on me that the man and the house were one. But as I was only about five at the time, I didn't think of such things. Instead, my eyes were riveted on a stick the old man clutched in his gnarled hands. It, too, was gnarled, bony, and hooked. The stick seemed to be an extension of the man, somehow like a branch of a tree. Just then a breeze tumbled down. The "branch" swayed. Terror grabbed my heart and I fled.

A few days passed before I gained courage to go back; by then, my curiosity was stronger than my fear. I crossed the village and followed the almost invisible footpath to his house. Few people passed that way. Once again I came upon the clearing and rounded the house. There he sat cross-legged in exactly the same position as I had last seen him. He tightly clutched the hooked stick, a vague resemblance to the witch in *Hansel and Gretel*. I was so sure that he could merely put out the stick and hook me with it that I kept my distance. How many days I spied on him I do not remember. Every day he sat in the same place and hardly moved. I suppose he would never have known I was around if one day I hadn't dared to venture within a few feet of him. He looked up, startled, and it wasn't until later that I knew he was blind. I did know, however, that his eyes had a grotesque blank stare, and once again I turned to run. But his words stopped me. *"Nanahnoe, aiq seno.* [My little friend, you've come.]" His words were low, slurred, but in that moment I knew in my childish way that he was my friend. I understood his quiet words, his toothless smile.

We talked. He was old, so he understood the young. He kept me intrigued for hours on end, spinning his stories of days when he was a great warrior, a great hunter, and a great man. The battles, the wild pig hunts, the sorrows, the joys: he told me about them all, not on just that first day, but every day. At times he seemed a frail twig—a twig that had been carved on but hadn't quite snapped. But more often I saw him as he used to be, strong and vibrant with life. His outer strength may have wasted away but not his inner strength. What were five broken fingers, a smashed nose, or his many scars?

"Life is like an arrow," he told me. "At one time it is new, but with every flight it takes upward toward a bird, there is the chance that it may miss and plunge to earth and perish in the rain forest. An arrow becomes old, and the more nicks it has in it, the more valued it is. But one day it is covered with nicks and it is too frail and old to send off into the air any more. So it is no longer taken out hunting, but it stays at home and becomes a memory. It may snap, but the memory will always keep on living—somewhere."

He was content with his life but he also realized something was missing. Sometimes I could detect a longing in his voice to be young again, to see once more the rugged beauty of the mountains, to hunt in the dense rain forest, to run home exultant, shouting across the valley in a song of triumph.

"Jesus healed blind people," I told him.

"Jesus?" He looked blank, and then, "Isn't that the swear word the patrol officers used to yell when they got mad?"

He did not know that Jesus was God or that Jesus loved him. So I told him about Jesus' great love. He would ask me, "Can Jesus make me see again?" And in childlike faith I would answer, yes, Jesus could make him see again.

The years passed. Most of the time I was away at school, but whenever it was vacation time I could hardly wait to see him again.

One day he said to me, "Some day, my little friend, I will know what you look like because soon Jesus is going to make me see again." I was older then, and my faith was not what it used to be. But I didn't say anything. After that he never asked any more whether Jesus would heal him. He didn't need to.

Vacation fled and then came again. I returned home and followed the path to the clearing where he would be waiting for me. But when I rounded the hut he was not there. The leaf had fallen. Another arrow had snapped, but I knew the memory would keep on living. Suddenly I realized what he had meant when he said that Jesus would heal him; that he would see me some day. He would be running at Jesus' side across the green fields, recognizing me and shouting my name.

PRAYER

Father, thank You for teachers and friends who have influenced our lives and the lives of our loved ones—our parents, our children, our brothers and sisters....

TO MEDITATE ON

Whatever you do, work at it with all your heart, as working for the Lord, not for men, since you know you will receive an inheritance from the Lord as a reward. It is the Lord Christ you are serving. (Colossians 3:23–24)

TO ASK MYSELF

Am I influencing the lives of people I come into contact with? Could I serve the Lord overseas as a teacher or as a children's home parent and thus have input into the lives of MKs?

---

* *Not in the Common Mould* by Lynette Oates chronicles David's colorful and inspiring life. This book is available from JAARS Center, Resource Room, Box 248, Waxhaw, NC 28173, or from Wycliffe Media, Graham Road, Kangaroo Grounds, VIC 3097, Australia.

19.

That One-More-Time Bomb

> Strong parents, like strong runners, have found that if they can persevere past the point of near exhaustion, a smoother going often follows. Stamina is a core quality of successful parenting.
> —Dr. Ray Guarendi

OUR DAUGHTERS NEVER LEFT us to go to a boarding school; rather *we* were the ones who left. We left Ukarumpa to go to the village to live among the Awas. Our daughters stayed at the Ukarumpa center in a children's home while we were gone.

It may appear that I'm speaking euphemistically. But to Ed and me, and to our daughters, there was a big difference.

Each time before we left for the village, Karen and Treesa talked excitedly about the home they would live in for the next two or so months. They would discuss who they would room with, what the new children's home parents would be like, where they would keep the key to our center house so they could come in and practice piano. Living in a children's home was always a new and exciting venture for them.

Each week, or more often if they wished, the girls talked to us by two-way radio for fifteen minutes. It became apparent after only one conversation that each needed her own fifteen-minute time slot!

We learned that despite being apart for weeks at a time, we remained a close family. One significant factor in our cohesiveness was our collected-through-the-years "family language." That language helped us deal with—

That One-More-Time Bomb

If he does that one more time, I'll clobber him!

Have you ever felt that way about something someone did? Articles by the dozen have been written on how to deal with such near-explosive feelings.

"Stop and count to ten," says one. Another also suggests you count. "Like the old hymn tells us, 'Count your many blessings one by one.'"

So you count: mere numbers or manifold blessings. You count to ten, twenty, thirty. And it helps—until another "one more time" ticks around.

If it's your children who are setting your fuse afire, various people's advice helps (or does it?).

Your mother's words console you. "I don't understand it. When *you* were a child, you were never the least bother," she reminisces.

That helps, for you interpret her words to mean, "I've completely forgotten what a little rascal you were!" So you are inspired with the hope that you, too, will forget—if you live through that "one more time" without exploding.

Friends offer advice, varied and inconsistent.

A neighbor woman, an ex-sergeant in the Air Force, exhorts, "Be firm with them!" So you try the old military tactic. And for a while your children march; they turn left, they turn right. Alas! You sometimes call "Right!" when you mean "Left!" You eventually decide you weren't cut out to be a drill sergeant.

"Just ignore them!" This gem of advice comes from a laid-back friend whose children are as passive as lily-studded ponds at dawn. But yours? More like rushing mountain streams: active, turbulent, alive with activity.

And so it goes, on and on. You're angry at your children or another member of your family. Or you're angry with a friend or coworker. And you wonder, *How can I defuse my anger?*

We discovered something that worked better for our family than the counting technique, better than the hope that "I too will forget," better than the "Be firm!" military maneuver, and much better than the "Just ignore them!" tactic. After all, you can ignore lilies floating on a pond, but who can ignore boulders and uprooted trees tumbling down a swift mountain stream when you're standing in the middle of that stream? That "something" you, too, can make work as you adapt it to your situation.

During Karen's and Treesa's growing-up years, we collected a "family language." Not just Mommy, but Daddy and the girls, too, found these *"frazes for frazzled tempers"* (as I'll call them) effective in defusing anger. The first, "Don't do dat!" you read about in Chapter 5.

Another family *fraze* came via Karen when she was four. One evening, her dad and I were heatedly *discussing* an issue. What it was I've forgotten. "You're inconsistent," I accused. "You're saying something that you yourself don't do."

Karen, exhibiting the zeal of Judge Wapner to see justice prevail, pronounced, "You's a hippo-kit, Daddy! You's a hippo-kit!" Where she picked that up, we don't know. Hypocrite is not a word we used in our family. But nevertheless, "You's a hippo-kit!" became part of our family language!

"You're *piribahri*!" was another of our family *frazes*. It wasn't until Karen said "You're *piribahri*!" to one of her Ukarumpa High School classmates that she discovered *piribahri* (pronounced peedy-body) was an Awa word, not an English word as she had thought for years. Through my and Ed's use of it, she had learned it meant "pigheaded," "stubborn," "unbending"—but because it was not in our mother tongue, it didn't have the sting those words have in English!

When visiting in Treesa and Michael's home, I've heard one of them say to the other, "You's an old beah (bear)." I've also noticed that said phrase elicits a smile.

Ed and I have added a new family-couple *fraze* to our repertoire. Close friends Drs. Edward and Carolyn Blight have been partners with us in Bible translation for many years. Dr. Ed has a tremendous sense of humor. He recently amused us with tales from his practice. (He was careful to keep names and specific facts that could identify a patient anonymous.) Some people, he says, continually doubt his evaluation of the prognosis of their illness and the need, or lack thereof, for treatment. "No matter what I say, I'm challenged with, 'But you don't *really* know, do you?'"

"No," he answers, "I don't *really* know, but given the statistics and the stage of your illness, I'd say...."

"But you don't *really* know, do you?"

When I am becoming overassertive, a trait to which my husband would normally react, he now chooses, rather, to challenge me with, "But you don't *really* know, do you?" And, of course, we think back to Dr. Ed's stories. My overassertive attitude goes out the window; Ed's tendency to react vanishes!

Yes, long ago in our home, when tempers flared and one of us felt *If she (or he) does that one more time,* how handy it was to spout out, "Don't do dat!" or "You's a hippo-kit!" or "You're *piribahri*!" It never failed to defuse the anger and, more often than not, left us all laughing.

It also opened the way to say "I love you" using our favorite family *fraze*. Treesa, the lover in our family, would sit on my lap and pat me on the cheeks expressing her love to me. "I zuv you, Mommy! I zuv you!"

"Oh, Treesa, I love you, too—a little bit," I teased one day.

"Oh, Mommy!" she shot back, "I zuv you zot, zot, z-o-o-t-t-t bit!"

"I zuv you zot, zot bit!" became firmly entrenched as part of our family language.

Today since our girls are grown and married, we have less use for our *frazes* to defuse anger. But we'll never outgrow the need to use our favorite *fraze*. Even emails from our girls often end with "Luv you zot, zot bit!" Love diffused across the continents.

PRAYER

God, help me to remember that when You said, "Be kind to each other," those "each others" include members of my family and my closest friend.

TO MEDITATE ON

Make sure that nobody pays back wrong for wrong, but always try to be kind to each other and to everyone else. (1 Thessalonians 5:15)

TO ASK MYSELF

Am I consistently defusing my anger toward others in a manner that glorifies God? Have I diffused love to someone today?

20.

A Time for Families

 Christmas is…a time for family
tradition, including wonderful
food, reunions, games, gifts,
decorations…prayers, children,
children and more children.
—Dr. James Dobson

THERE COMES A TIME when the missionary family go on furlough
knowing they will return as only "half a family."

Karen graduated from high school in 1977. We had extended our
normal five-year field term an extra six months so that she could graduate from Ukarumpa High School with her class. Once again, it had
been five and a half years since either Ed's mother or my mother had
seen her granddaughters. But neither complained. God blessed both
me and Ed with mothers who respected God's call on our lives.

It was good for us all to be in the USA with Karen that first year
of her settling into college life. Great to have her "home" with us for
holidays. The year went all too fast. I felt as though my heart would
ache out of my body as we waved goodbye after the last weekend visit
with her on campus. We would return overseas and face our first
Christmas as a family of three.

Those first weeks back in Papua New Guinea were not without tears. In another year and a half, Ed and I would take Treesa to the USA for college, stay a few short months, and then return alone to PNG.

That first year apart from us, Karen wrote "A Missionary Daughter's Prayer," which was translated into German and published in the German WBT newsletter. Later it was published in *Psychology for Living* with the title "A Time for Families." After reading that article, we learned what a commitment our Karen had to our work of translating the Bible for the Awa people. We also learned that her first year away from us was not at all an easy time for her. Especially Christmas, which is—

A Time for Families

Christmas is just around the corner, God. All around I see hustle and bustle—the Christmas shoppers, the brightly decorated store windows, tinseled trees, colored lights, carolers. Oh, there's excitement in the air. There's a feeling of secrecy, a feeling of expectation for Christmas morning.

And God, my heart aches because it is also a time for families, a time to be together, to share love and oneness.

But God, I can't be with my family this Christmas. My roommates and friends here on campus talk about "going home." But I can't go home to my family. I won't see Dad and Mom and my little sister this Christmas. I really want to rejoice with them that they're out there telling people that You love them, God. But it's hard to rejoice when underneath you just plain hurt. And right now, I just plain hurt. I'm so far away from my family, and I might not even get a chance to talk to them. Telephone service there is so unreliable. Help me remember, God, that physical separation can't break the oneness of our family. They love me. Distance will never change that.

Also help me remember, Father, that they are where You want them to be, and that I'm here in college where You want me. The time comes when a child is not really any longer a child. And You know that because of the difference in school systems there and here, I started my education young; so that time came extra early for me. But even though I'm grown up—O God, right now I don't feel grown up; I'm crying and I just want to be home where a child ought to be at Christmas! But as I was saying, God, even though I'm grown, and I've had to be separated from my family, we're still a family because we love each other. Help me to remember that, God.

And, God, help me remember the true meaning of Christmas. That first Christmas for You was a time of love. You loved us so much that You sent us a Gift, Your only Son. You sent Him down to become one of us. He walked the earth and died for the sins of the world—and for my sins. Yes, that first Christmas was a time of love, but it was also a time when You were separated from Your only Son. You knew the pain and sorrow He would go through, and that caused You pain. You knew people would turn their backs on Your Gift. You knew they'd mock Him and kill Him. You ached because, for a time, You were going to have to turn Your back on Him, too.

Yes, Father God, Christmas was a time of real love and pain for You. Help me to remember that, as this Christmas I experience just a tiny bit of Your pain. Yes, God, I hurt. But I know my parents love me. I'm glad, though, that they love You more. They're willing to be apart from me so a group of people who have never read the Christmas story in their own language will be able to read it this Christmas.

PRAYER

Father, as Karen prayed, we also pray: Help us remember the true meaning of Christmas, not just at the Christmas season but through-out the year. Stir our hearts to feel concern for those who have never read or never even heard the Christmas story in their own language.

TO MEDITATE ON

This is love: not that we loved God, but that he loved us and sent his Son as an atoning sacrifice for our sins. (1 John 4:10)

TO ASK MYSELF

Am I concerned and willing to sacrifice so that people will be able to read the Christmas story in their own language?

21.

Girl without a Country

 Your faithfulness extends to
every generation, as enduring
as the earth you created.
—Psalm 119:90 NLT

"HELLO, THIS IS ARETTA LOVING." We were in Southern California, so
I took the opportunity to phone the Wycliffe Associates (WA)* office.

"Oh, I know *you*! You're Karen Loving's mother," the woman on
the other end of the line exclaimed.

"Now I know how Karen and Treesa feel," I later told Ed. Before
Ed and I met, he had worked three years on college campuses in the
southeast USA encouraging Christians in their walk with the Lord.
Our daughters were often greeted at InterVarsity Christian Fellowship
conferences with, "Oh, you must be the daughters of Ed and Aretta
Loving!"

The woman on the phone went on to tell me about "that wonderful article Karen had written." With that article, Karen had won
an MK contest sponsored by *In Other Words*, Wycliffe USA's publication. People at the WA office were setting up an Uncle-Auntie program for Wycliffe MKs coming home to enter college. Karen's article

highlighted the need for MKs to have "relatives" near them, the woman on the phone told me. WA reprinted Karen's article and sent it out to their mailing list. Not only did Karen gain enough notoriety for me to be referred to as "Karen Loving's mother," she also received a fifty dollar prize, money she needed for an urgent college expense and had prayed that God would supply.

In that article we saw once again our daughter's commitment to the Lord, even in the midst of the trauma she faced her first year after leaving New Guinea. In the following article Karen tells us that she felt like a—

Girl without a Country

Numbly I stood watching the car drive off into the distance. All that was familiar was fast disappearing over the horizon. I dreaded the moment when I would have to turn around and walk up the stairs into the gymnasium where registration was being held. I wanted to run after the car and cry, "Take me home. I don't belong here!" but I couldn't move. Although this campus was to be my new home, I knew it could never take the place of what I called home.

Home was Ukarumpa, our center in Papua New Guinea, an island that most of these students around me had never heard of. I was born in PNG and had lived there until just a few weeks before, when I'd graduated from Ukarumpa High School. Mom, Dad, and my younger sister came back with me and stayed in the States during my first year of college.

I thought back over the many happy years of life in New Guinea and longed for familiar faces and for Pudgy, my dog. Pudgy had understood my every mood. Here no one understood me. I was a foreigner; the only bond between me and the USA was my citizenship. In my heart, I felt that was a very weak bond.

Finally, I pulled myself away from my thoughts and began to notice the activity around me. Everyone seemed to know what to do except me, and I was too scared to ask. I'd heard horror stories about college registration. I was not looking forward to entering that gym. A long line was forming before the door and not wanting to look conspicuous, I stepped to the end of it.

"Eleven o'clock registration. Last call for eleven o'clock registration!" I looked at the computer card in my hand and realized that was my time. Hurrying to the door, I fought my way into the gym. College life had begun for me.

During the next few weeks I had so many new experiences that I often felt confused and out of place. The five girls I lived with were not Christians. One roommate was involved with a married man. One spent five or six nights a week at her boyfriend's place. One later eloped, another became pregnant, and the fifth was fast becoming an alcoholic. Growing up in Papua New Guinea in a Christian community, I'd never encountered problems like these.

How different from our teachers in PNG were my professors! They didn't seem to care about the students. Most acted as though they thought teaching was a chore. Classes were large and impersonal. Students in my English class were always talking about "Star Wars," which everyone except me had seen. They also talked about various rock music groups and movies. I had no clue what they were talking about.

In the dining hall I couldn't eat because of all the activity and noise around me. At home meal times had always been quiet and unhurried. I had never seen so many people eating together at one time—and so fast!

Grocery stores and department stores were so big and confusing. In New Guinea shopping had been easy. There wasn't much choice. You bought what was there or you didn't buy. Even crossing the street in the States seemed a terrifying experience. Cars whizzed by. In New Guinea the few cars moved at a slow pace over the rutted, dirt roads. The coastal cities we visited once a year didn't have enough cars on the roads to even merit stoplights!

But the one thing I dreaded most was the age-old question, "Where are you from?" I didn't really know. I'd left New Guinea behind me, probably never to see it again, to begin a new phase of my life. School was definitely not my home, and it was too early in my stateside experience to feel that Grandma's farm, several hours away, was home. I felt like a person without a country.

I made lots of friends, and outwardly, I seemed happy and well adjusted. But inside, constant turmoil caused me to feel confused, lonely, fearful, and homesick. My friends didn't know or understand the real Karen Loving. The only thing I looked forward to were the weekends, when I could go to my grandmother's or be with my parents while they were visiting churches and speaking.

I learned quickly that my life depended on the early morning "meetings," when I'd find a quiet place and spend time with God. I dreaded each new day, but as I took it to the Lord, He gave me the strength to meet the tasks before me.

"Karen, I was a stranger among My people. I was alone and yet not alone. The crowds followed Me and so did My twelve disciples, but they didn't understand Me or My purpose, or where I'd come from. But My Father was always there, just as I am always here when you need Me."

For the first time in my life I began to understand a little of what Christ's coming to earth really meant. I could identify with His feeling of loneliness. Christ had gone through so much; He understood, and I knew He could help me. I gave Him my confusion, loneliness, fear, homesickness, and culture shock. In their place He began to fill me with love and peace. Things didn't change overnight, but He was always there guiding me over the rough spots, comforting me in my times of homesickness, and being a friend in times of loneliness.

A couple of years have passed, and I've changed schools. I'm finishing my third year of nursing and now I love college. Yet I'm still a foreigner here. Will the United States ever be home to me? I don't know. But I do know that I have a perfect home waiting for me in heaven and a loving Father guiding me day by day until I reach that perfect home!

PRAYER

Lord, changes *are* difficult! When I embark on some new venture in obedience to You, help me to realize that You go right along with me on that venture.

TO MEDITATE ON

The LORD had said to Abram, "Leave your country, your people and your father's household and go to the land I will show you.... Do not be afraid.... I am your shield, your very great reward. (Genesis 12:1, 15:1)

TO ASK MYSELF

Do I sometimes feel that when I get on a plane for a cross-country trip, God stays behind at the airport? Or am I aware that He embarks with me, sits beside me, and holds my hand all the way, then disembarks along with me at the end of the journey?

---

* See Appendix G.

22.

God's Ways Are Not Always Logical

It may be only a pinpoint on the map but if it is the Lord's place for us, it is a large place. God's geography does not read like ours. His ways are not our ways and His standards of greatness and success are foolish to this world.
—Vance Havner

THE AWA NEW TESTAMENT was dedicated in Papua New Guinea in 1974, and Ed and I were serving our coworkers while living at Ukarumpa. Ed managed the Technical Studies Department, which oversees the disciplines of language and culture learning, anthropology research, literacy, and translation. I worked under him as manager and editor of *READ*, a literacy-literature magazine published in Papua New Guinea and mailed to countries all over the world.

Karen was in the States attending college. Treesa was in her senior year of high school. Surely it was logical that we continue to live at Ukarumpa until she graduated. We would then take her to the USA for college. But Treesa's unselfish attitude and love for God helped us realize that to us—

God's Ways Are Not Always Logical

"Would you consider coming out to the Sepik* and serving as our director?" colleagues asked Ed.

The Sepik—hot and humid. But that was not the reason Ed said no. "Not now. In six months from now Treesa graduates from high school, and then she'll leave the nest. We feel we ought to be here with her until then," was his reply to our coworkers.

For almost twenty years we'd lived and worked in the highlands. After finishing the Awa New Testament, we began serving our fellow translators on the technical side of things, at the same time completing a book of Old Testament Bible stories in Awa. We'd been at Ukarumpa while Karen finished high school. Now Treesa....

"Wait!" the Lord seemed to say. "Have you considered asking Me what My will is?"

"Well, now that You mention it, Lord, no. But we thought it was logical."

"But My ways are not always logical to *your* mind, you know!"

At last we told the Lord we were willing to take that administrative assignment away from Ukarumpa, though it wasn't what we really wanted to do at that time. We wanted to stay with Treesa while she finished high school. But we began to ask God whether moving to the Sepik was indeed His plan for us. We talked it over with Treesa.

"Why don't you accept the offer, Dad? You'd enjoy that work. And Mom, you know you'd enjoy the warmer climate," was her instant response.

As we prayed, we began to want to do the very thing to which we'd first said no.

We left our lovely highland house at Ukarumpa with the new wall-to-wall living room carpet, a gift from one of our supporting churches. More than missing that carpet, we would miss the PNG young people from the nearby Aiyura National High School. Each Saturday evening they came to our home. Sitting cross-legged, they filled every square inch of available space on that carpet. We worshiped the Lord in song together. A number would lead out in meaningful prayers. The students listened with rapt attention as Ed taught truths from God's Word. God moved deeply in the lives of many of this cream-of-the-crop group.

Nevertheless, we left our home and those young people behind. We left Treesa in Teen Manor, one of the children's homes, under the loving care of house parents Cam and Marj Goodwin. As parents of out-of-the-nest children in the USA, the Goodwins had responded to God's call from the PNG branch to come over and help us.

We left the cool climate and the warm fellowship of close friends. We left work assignments at Ukarumpa that had to be eventually filled by translators who had to lay aside their work on the New Testament for a while.

But what did we gain? The fun and excitement of administrative treks up the mighty Sepik River by riverboat and dugout canoe. Sometimes we flew by helicopter or small plane over miles of green-velvet jungle. Other times Ed drove a four-wheel-drive vehicle on muddy roads and through flooded rivers. Or sometimes we mushed our way through swamps, then trod narrow, slippery trails punctuated by swinging vine bridges—or worse, mere poles wedged across rivers. Neither of the latter was a problem to Ed. He would nonchalantly walk across them as though he had once been part of a tightrope-walking act. But I am not endowed with that same sense of balance. On single-pole spans I used a more down-to-earth approach. "The seat of your trousers is going to catch and rip on that pole! Then where will we buy you a new pair?" Ed often teased.

Oh, the relief we always felt upon reaching our destination safely and being met by coworkers with a *kulau* (a drinking coconut) and a serving of luscious tropical fruit. The greatest gain, though, was the satisfaction of helping and encouraging teams as they struggled to finish New Testaments.

Yes, we gained by our move! But should that surprise us? Doesn't God's Word promise that if we delight ourselves in Him, He will give us the desires of our hearts? We've found that He even creates those desires, if necessary, so that He can give them to us.

PRAYER

Lord, help me to remain flexible and willing to move when You say "Get up! Time to move." Your Word in Psalm 37:4 admonishes me to "delight yourself in the LORD and he will give you the desires of your heart." Help me realize that You really do give me the desires of my heart when I submit my will to Yours.

TO MEDITATE ON

I am the LORD your God, who teaches you what is best for you, who directs you in the way you should go. (Isaiah 48:17)

We can make our plans, but the LORD determines our steps. (Proverbs 16:9 NLT)

He brought me forth also into a large place....He delighted in me. (Psalm 18:19 KJV)

TO ASK MYSELF

Am I willing for God to change the desires of my heart so they become synonymous with His desires?

---

* The Sepik River is to Papua New Guinea what the Amazon River is to Brazil. "The Sepik" is short for the East Sepik Province and the Sundaun Province (formerly the West Sepik Region). At the time my husband was asked to be director there, about thirty translation teams, one literacy team, and support workers servicing four regional centers made up the Sepik team.

23.

Jesus Does "Like Light Does"

> The key thing about light is that its radiance can best be seen in the darkest places.
> —Chuck Colson

"WHY DIDN'T YOU SEND your daughters to a Bible school instead of to secular universities?" many of our friends asked us.

Our daughters were in "Bible school" from kindergarten through high school at our Ukarumpa center schools. If they were to stand for the Lord in our home culture, they surely would find a secular university the perfect proving ground. And we knew that God was able to protect them spiritually. This was proven to us when I learned that—

Jesus Does "Like Light Does"

Karen was in her second year at the University of Virginia. We prayed for her, as is our custom for each of our two daughters, daily. "Lord, keep her safe spiritually and physically." She wrote that she had joined the Nurses Christian Fellowship, an arm of InterVarsity Christian Fellowship. God was answering our prayers for her spiritual safety.

Then she wrote saying she had a night class from 7 to 9 p.m. twice weekly. "Pray for me, Mom and Dad. To get back to the dorm, I walk down a street called 'Rape Street.' There are no houses on either side of the street, and at night it's sorta dark. A lot of girls are grabbed and...."

My heart jumped into my throat, and I found it difficult to read the rest of that sentence. Even if a nickname, what a horrible name for a street!

"O Lord," I cried out, "protect our daughter. Surround her with Yourself. Be with her, be all around her." Her dad and I took in account the time difference and prayed especially hard for her on the days she had that night class and would be walking down Rape Street!

One morning in my daily devotions I read Jesus' words, "I am the light of the world."

What do those words mean? I pondered. "Lord, I don't really understand how You are light."

In Karen's next letter she wrote, "When I come back to my dorm after my night classes, I walk down the middle of the street, because there I'm surrounded by light on all sides."

I then understood what "God is light" meant. A back-to-English translation of John 3:19 from the Awa New Testament reads, "The One who does like light does came down to earth." I had peace in my heart that God had heard our prayers. He was protecting Karen, surrounding her on all sides "like light does."

PRAYER

O Lord, Light of the world, we really can trust our loved ones into Your hands!

TO MEDITATE ON

God took care of me when he lighted the way before me and I walked safely through the darkness. (Job 29:2–3 TLB)

TO ASK MYSELF

Why do I worry, when God controls the future? Will I choose to trust Him for my loved ones, knowing that "the One who does like light does came down to earth," and He's with them?

24.

Heartbreak

 God can do wonders with a
broken heart if you give him
all the pieces.
—Victor Alfsen

I HAVE LEARNED THAT sometimes it is hard—very hard—to follow
God. But I echo the words of Simon Peter, "Master, to whom shall we
go? You alone have the words that give eternal life, and we believe
them and know that you are the holy Son of God" (John 6:68–69 TLB).

So I am committed to following Him even if that entails—

Heartbreak

How could she leave him, one she had grown to love so much? He
had come into her life while she was home on furlough. And now that
time was coming to an end. But, *Oh*, her heart cried out, *how can I leave
him? How can I? Africa—so far away, so very far away from him.*

Yet she was committed to serving God, and that meant returning
overseas. Returning and leaving him, even though she felt her heart
was breaking.

As she packed, her thoughts went back to the first time she'd seen him. For her, it had been the proverbial love at first sight. But he hadn't even noticed her, hadn't even smiled at her. Most would have considered him unattractive; some might have described him as ugly.

She couldn't explain why she felt such an attraction to him. In the months since she'd first seen him, he'd not shown her much attention. Once in a while he smiled at her, and at those times it seemed he felt the same about her as she did about him. Yet mostly he ignored her. Still she loved him more and more each day, and her heart was breaking at the thought of leaving him. But the bottom line was that even though she loved him deeply, she loved God more. So she was returning to her work overseas.

She would count the months, forty-eight of them. And she would write him that many letters, knowing that the precious few communications she received from him would be, at the most, only quickly scribbled pieces. And she would tick off the four long years one by one and dream of the time she'd return—return to him. He would meet her at the airport. She could see him running toward her, reaching his arms out to her. He would greet her with, "I love you, Gwa'ma!"

Jesus said, "And everyone who has left...children...for my sake will receive a hundred times as much and will inherit eternal life" (Matthew 19:29).

And she asked, "Lord, *grand*children, too?"

And He whispered to her heart, "Lovest thou Me more than these?"

"Yes, Lord, I love You," she said with tears in her eyes. "I'll go."

And she went.

PRAYER

Lord Jesus, I do love You more than anyone or anything! And if Your working out Your purpose and plan in my life involves a heartbreak, I accept that heartbreak and even thank You for it.

TO MEDITATE ON

A broken...heart, O God, you will not despise. (Psalm 51:17)

A bruised reed he will not break, and a smoldering wick he will not snuff out, till he leads justice to victory. (Matthew 12:20)

He healeth the broken in heart, and bindeth up their wounds. (Psalm 147:3 KJV)

And everyone who has left houses or brothers or sisters or father or mother or children or fields for my sake will receive a hundred times as much and will inherit eternal life. (Matthew 19:29)

TO ASK MYSELF

Is my love for anyone or anything keeping me from following God's will for my life?

25.

Would I Mess Up an Opportunity? Or Would I Turn a Mess Into an Opportunity?

Lord, don't let me make
a mess of things.
—Psalm 119:31b TLB

YES, WE WENT TO AFRICA, and left a new grandson in the USA.

After finishing the translation of the New Testament, our director in Papua New Guinea had asked us to think about transferring to Africa. The need there for experienced workers, he said, was great.

"Not now. Our daughters are still in high school. We'll reconsider it once they graduate," we told him.

Now our "reconsider Africa" time had come. And it didn't take us long to decide that we did not want to go there. We enjoyed administering the thirty-plus translation, literacy, and support teams from the small Sepik River region center.

Then the doctor in the small town across the river from the center there in the Sepik diagnosed Ed's chest pains as angina! "Go south {to Australia} for a specific diagnosis and treatment," he advised.

Instead of going "south," we decided to go to the USA. We left the most pleasant climate in the world: hot days and cool, one-sheet-weather nights. We'd miss the most delicious food in the world: tropical fruit par excellence! We closed the door on the most beautiful house in the world: a thatch-roofed, wire-screened porchlike house overlooking a valley of swaying bamboo and sago palms. We both felt we might never again open the door to that house where we had spent some of the happiest years of our "after Karen and Treesa left the nest" lives!

Our daughter Karen had worked at the University of Virginia Hospital in Charlottesville. She lined up a cardiologist to see her dad. A treadmill test showed no heart problems. More tests revealed a hiatal hernia—which by that time had quieted down.

While home in the States, we were again asked to consider an assignment in East Africa. The Lord had gotten our attention! Now we were willing and ready to go to Africa!

In Kenya we served under the national organization, Bible Translation and Literacy (BTL), East Africa.* Ed, as the language programs coordinator, supervised all translation programs, about half of which were headed up by Kenyans. I worked as a writer and editor. We served under the best "boss" we've ever had: Micah Amukobole, a wonderful man of God. I had the privilege of working closely with BTL's public relations coordinator—a fun person to work with! Mundara Muturi is dedicated to BTL's vision: to see the smaller language groups of Kenya receive God's Word in their mother tongue. (The Bible Society works in the larger language groups in Kenya.)

Besides having a Kenyan boss and colleagues, we had Wycliffe colleagues from the USA, Canada, England, Germany, Australia, the Netherlands, Ireland, Switzerland, Finland, South Africa, and Denmark.

For many years Iver and Alice Larsen were the only Danish members in Wycliffe. Since Alice and I share a love of writing (and she did a very creditable job of editing my English manuscripts!), we became fast friends. Alice was the mother of Jakob (pronounced Yah-kob) and Heidi and teenagers Thomas and Ann Brit. Alice allowed me to write her story in which she asks—

Would I Mess Up an Opportunity?
Or Would I Turn a Mess Into an Opportunity?

"Jakob, I'm leaving Sneakers in your care," our daughter Ann said as she placed her pet hamster in Jakob's arms. "Take good care of Sneakers while I'm at boarding school," she commissioned her five-year-old brother as she hugged him goodbye.

Jakob was thrilled to be appointed chief hamster warden. Sneakers was carried wherever Jakob went, outside and inside.

Alas! Jakob's mother did not share Jakob's enthusiasm. "I'm fed up with the smell and the mess! An animal's place is not in the house. This animal ought to be played with only outside on the grass," I complained. Then in my thoughts I added, *And maybe he'll run away and be gone from my life forever!*

The next day Jakob burst into the house wailing as though someone had beaten him—or as though.... Oh, no! Could it be...?

Jakob and Heidi had played with Sneakers outside on the grass all morning. *Has my "maybe" wish come true?* I thought guiltily.

Sneakers was gone. It was now my time to wail—inwardly. *Had my negative attitude contributed to his disappearance?*

"Jakob, let's go out and look for Sneakers," I offered.

Jakob, Heidi, and I, joined by neighbor children, searched under, behind, around, in, and even on top of every bush where a small creature could possibly hide. Our search flushed out missing toys, an old bird nest, some fat spiders, and lizards—but no hamster.

As I put my arms around a weeping Jakob, the Holy Spirit reminded me, "Haven't you been looking for opportunities to help Jakob and Heidi experience God in their lives? What are you going to do about this? Will you let your dislike for a mess keep them from seeing Me work?"

I managed to push aside my "but what if God doesn't...?" doubts. "Let's ask God to help us find Sneakers," I said, hoping the Holy Spirit would slip some small seed of faith into my heart as I prayed.

Jakob thought that was a great idea! My prayer was short, and I wondered how sincere I was. "Dear God, please help Jakob to find Sneakers. Amen."

Again we went outside and searched. Still no Sneakers.

But Jakob wasn't ready to give up on God. Oh, no. He felt we needed to do more than ask God to help us find Sneakers. "We need to tell God that He must find Sneakers and put him back in his cage!"

"When we pray, we don't command God; we ask Him," I reminded my son. "How do you think God will find him? And how is He going to 'put him back in the cage'?" I asked. That tiny seed of faith I had asked for was being stretched to the bursting point.

Heidi, with a three-year-old's enthusiastic faith, piped up with her explanation. "God will see him and put him back in the cage, and then He'll go back up in the air."

Jakob thought about that a minute. "Well, I don't think God will come down and find Sneakers Himself. But I think He will tell him to get out from under the bushes so somebody can find him and put him in his cage."

And with that, Jakob and Heidi (*trusting little souls that they are*, I thought with envy) ran outside to play with their friends who had congregated to help look for Sneakers.

As I went about my household chores, I pondered my children's faith. Could I lay aside my intense dislike of their pet's mess and really believe with them? How would God honor their faith?

About an hour later a knock interrupted my thoughts. I opened the door, and there stood Johnny, a neighbor boy, with Sneakers in his arms. Passing by on the way to the playground, he had spied Sneakers peeking out from behind a bush. I thanked Johnny profusely. I didn't tell him that he was a live "angel"—a messenger, at least—sent by God to help Him get Sneakers back in his cage.

That night after I'd tucked Jakob in, he slipped out of bed and came to me. "Mommy, I was excited to come in and find Sneakers right there in his cage—'cause God helped Johnny find him and helped you put him in his cage. It's good that we prayed, isn't it?"

"Yes, Jakob," I agreed. "We should always remember to pray."

As I lay down to sleep, I knew God had not only taught my children that He cared about their concerns; He had also taught this mother that it was important not to *mess up an opportunity* to teach her children to trust Him. In fact, far more important than avoiding a stinky mess!

PRAYER

Lord, grant me wisdom to know that a child is more important than my dislike of a mess.

TO MEDITATE ON

So I say to you: Ask and it will be given to you; seek and you will find; knock and the door will be opened to you. (Luke 11:9)

TO ASK MYSELF

Am I letting my hang-ups (legitimate or not) keep me or those in my family from experiencing God at work in my life and theirs?

---

* See Appendix H.

26.

Two Brothers and Two Eggs

> We love Him because He is our Savior, and we *fear and reverence Him* because He knows all about us and knows all that is in us....
> —A. W. Tozer (emphasis mine)

A LITTLE MAN—IN STATURE, that is. From birth the odds were against Zaccheaus. But God in His great mercy....

Zaccheaus was born two months prematurely, still encased in the amniotic sac. His Tharaka people of Kenya believed that such an aberrant birth made him unworthy of a burial. "This thing," they decided, must be cast out to the hyenas to be shredded by sharp, hungry teeth or thrown to the cattle to be trampled under hoof. After that they would sacrifice an animal to appease the spirits.

But God in His great mercy moved in the heart of the baby's elderly aunt. It was she who saved Zaccheaus's life. And later, this aunt revealed the mystery that enshrouded the events of his birth just as tightly as the sac of water enshrouded his body. As Zaccheaus was about to be thrown into the cattle yard, his aunt reached out and snatched him—just in time. "No, this one shall not be trampled under the hooves of the cattle!" she insisted.

Zaccheaus lived, but he was a weak and sickly little boy. His class-mates taunted him by calling him *Nithimba*. A *nithimba* is a small rodentlike animal similar to a porcupine. These animals ravish the gardens of Zaccheaus's people. Corn is their favorite food. Despite the volume of corn an ugly little *nithimba* eats, he never grows fat.

Zaccheaus's wife, Stella, is glad he wasn't thrown to the hyenas when he was born.

In the mid-1960s, when Zaccheaus was fifteen, missionaries from a Norwegian-based mission established a church in his village. Zaccheaus heard the good news and became a believer in Jesus.

In early 1988, Zaccheaus resigned his job as principal of a Bible school and joined Bible Translation and Literacy (BTL) to head up the mother-tongue translation project in his Tharaka language. Our interaction with this personable young man whom Ed, in his role as language programs coordinator with BTL, supervised was not "all work and no play." If the BTL guest house was full, sometimes Zaccheaus would spend the night with us in our one-bedroom apartment, sleeping on our living room couch. Zaccheaus was a Scrabble player, and even though English was not his first language, he managed to beat me more than I beat him. Between games, he often told us legends of his Tharaka people.

Zaccheaus gave me permission to write one of the Tharaka legends. The best illustration I've ever heard of "the fear of the Lord" came from the legend called—

Two Brothers and Two Eggs

Long, long ago there lived an old man who had two sons, Naga and Mugao. One day the father called his two sons to him and gave each an egg. "Take your egg and find a place where no one can see you," the father told his sons. "Once you have found that place, crack your egg there, then return to me."

He told them that to find out whether they feared God.

Naga, the older son, took his egg and said to himself, *I will go and find a deep, dark cave—a cave so dark that not even the bats can see to fly about in it at night. In the darkness of that cave, no one will be able to see me. There I will crack my egg. My father will be pleased with me. He will think I am a good and clever son.*

He took his egg and left. He walked for many days. Finally he found a dark cave and went deep, deep inside it. There, thinking that no one could see him, he carefully cracked his egg. Then he returned home to his father, pleased with himself.

Mugao, the younger son, left with his egg and for many days wandered from place to place. But He found no place to crack his egg. So he returned to his father with his egg in hand.

"Father," Mugao said, "I traveled many days. I went here and I went there. I went to the tops of the highest mountains. I went to the lowest shores by the seas. I went into deep, dank caves and into dark, tangled forests. But I found no place where I could crack my egg. For although I found many places where no person could see me, I found no place where I could hide from God. I know God can see me even in the darkest, most secret place. So here is my egg. I can only return it to you uncracked."

"The father of a righteous man has great joy; he who has a wise son delights in him" (Proverbs 23:24).

PRAYER

Almighty God, not only are You omnipotent, You are omniscient; You are omnipresent. We sometimes forget that You are also our loving Father, and those big, theological words simply mean that You are all powerful (omnipotent), You know everything (omniscient), and You are everywhere (omnipresent). You know even our unspoken thoughts. You are able to see us at all times. Thank You.

TO MEDITATE ON

O LORD, you have searched me and you know me....You discern my going out and my lying down; you are familiar with all my ways....Where can I go from your Spirit? Where can I flee from your presence? (Psalm 139:1,3,7)

He who fears the LORD has a secure fortress, and for his children it will be a refuge. The fear of the LORD is a fountain of life. (Proverbs 14:26–27a)

TO ASK MYSELF

Like Mugao, the younger son, do I live in the knowledge that there is no place I can go and "crack my egg" where God does not see me?

27.

Cornered and Caught by an Angry Elephant

 Jesus Christ is no security
against storms. But He is
a perfect security in storms.
He has never promised
an easy passage. Only
a safe landing.
—Anonymous

DAVID DIIDA (PRONOUNCED DEEDA) was another young Kenyan man
whom Ed supervised in his role as language programs coordinator
with BTL. After Diida translated the Bible for his Borana people of
northern Kenya, he realized that "literacy is the key that unlocks
God's Word." About two years after we went to Kenya, he joined BTL
to work among the Borana people in literacy.

It became evident that the enemy wasn't pleased with Diida. In a
bus accident, steam from the engine severely burned Diida's ankles.
Another time, the bus Diida was traveling in was stopped by *shiftas*
(robbers), who stole all he had with him, including his briefcase with
literacy materials in it. Then when traveling to his home in northern
Kenya a huge elephant....

But here is that story (which he gave me permission to write for
him) told in his own words—

Cornered and Caught by an Angry Elephant

Well, Diida, this is the end, I said to myself as I lay there on the ground. The angry elephant was swinging his trunk around, trying to find me. I looked up at him and looked at myself and realized how hopeless my situation was. There was no way I could escape. I had run and lost the race. Death was only seconds away.

I thought about my wife and children. I had been gone from them for over a month, and they were now waiting for me at home. *How would Esther manage to raise four children alone? How would Tume, Guyyo, and Boru get along without a father? Galgalo, only six months old, would never even remember his father.*

It was mid-December, the time of the short rains in my part of Kenya. I had been in Nairobi making final corrections on the Borana Bible. Working under the Bible Society of Kenya in cooperation with the United Bible Societies, I had begun translating the Bible into my Borana language eleven years ago. Now as the year was coming to a close, I was encouraged. It would not be too many more months before my people would have God's Word in the language that spoke to their hearts!

Usually the trip home to Marsibit took only a day or two. I had planned to have time with my family before Christmas. But this year the rains had been heavier than usual, and in places the road had turned into a mass of mud. We had already had four overnights on the road. It was now past midday, and our bus driver was not willing to continue until the rain stopped and the road began drying up.

"It's only about fifteen miles from where we must leave the bus. Why don't we just walk the rest of the way?" a few of us decided. We are used to walking longer distances than that in our part of the country.

It was late afternoon when we set out. After walking about four miles, we came upon a huge elephant there in the Marsibit National Reserve close by the roadside. And he wasn't the kind that stands and eyes tourists with disinterest. This one was ready to attack! And we were ready to run. And run we did!

The elephant charged out of the bush after us, trumpeting his anger. *Such a large creature surely can't run too fast*, I thought. Wrong!

You would have thought we were training for a marathon. My lungs felt as though they would explode. My legs, like house stumps that termites had eaten the insides out of, threatened to collapse at any moment. I was second in the race, and I ran faster still—not to catch up with the person in first place, but because the elephant was gaining on us fast.

"Let's scatter into the bush," someone yelled. Our only hope was to leave the road and each of us try to find his own place of hiding. Just into the bush, I slipped and fell.

The elephant immediately abandoned his chase of the others and came for me. I scrambled to my feet and dashed into thicker bush, hoping to find a hiding place somewhere out there in the approaching darkness. The elephant was right behind me when I fell again. He began to search for me. Using his acute sense of smell, he raked his long trunk along the ground.

It was then that I said to myself, *Well, Diida, this is the end.* God reminded me to pray before I died. Bible heroes of faith came to mind. Daniel. God had rescued him from a den of lions. And Jonah. God took care of him in the rough sea and prepared a fish for him. Even inside the belly of that fish God was with him.

While looking up at the elephant with my eyes, my inner eyes were looking up to the Lord. "Lord, I know You control all things. You gave help to those men in the Bible, and I believe You can still give that kind of help today. I know You have all power. You are powerful enough to keep this elephant from killing me. But if it is Your will for me to die today out here in this wilderness, please accept my spirit into Your kingdom."

After praying, I received courage to once again believe that I might escape. *I'll crawl back behind him where he can't see me, then maybe I can get away before he turns around*, I thought.

But he heard me move. "Eh-eh-eh-eh!" he trumpeted. He dragged me over the rocks and stones, pushed me around some. Then his large trunk wrapped itself around my body, almost crushing me. He swung me into the air, then threw me on the ground.

"Lord God," I cried out, "I'm ready to die. Receive my spirit."

Hearing my voice seemed to infuriate the elephant even more. He picked me up again and threw me between his legs. But in his zeal, he overdid it. Miraculously, I landed not underneath his belly but behind him.

"I am not dead," I breathed. "I am still alive! But now I must do something quickly."

As the elephant snorted and stamped his feet trying to crush me, I crawled away into the darkness. I staggered back onto the road. Although my body ached all over and blood was oozing down my face, I made myself walk as fast as I could.

I saw a light coming toward me. A group of enemy warriors were soon standing face-to-face with me! I had escaped the elephant—and now this. I trembled as a flashlight blinded me. "What happened to you?" one of the men gasped.

I told them my story. The men had mercy on me and helped me get to people who took me to the hospital. X-rays showed no broken bones, and though my body was terribly bruised, my wounds were only superficial.

"I imagine you had nightmares after that," people say to me.

It's natural they would think that. But I've not suffered one bad dream over it. From the time I prayed lying there on the ground expecting to die, God encouraged me in a special way. He has given me a wonderful peace and a sense of awe that I'm alive.

I have also been asked, "Why do you think God spared your life?"

I don't know for sure. Maybe God wanted to test my faith as He did with Daniel. I believe that God has a plan for each of us, just as His Word says in Jeremiah 29:11: "I know the plans I have for you, plans to prosper you and not to harm you, plans to give you hope and a future." I know in my future there is more work for me to do. Once the Borana Bible is printed, people need to be able to read it. Bible

Translation and Literacy (BTL), East Africa, has invited me to head up the literacy work among my own people. I have committed myself to doing that.

Some people think miracles don't happen anymore. Some even doubt that God exists. But as for me, I really saw God do a miracle on my behalf. I was as good as dead. I had accepted the fact that I would die. God snatched me back from death; He gave me new life. Now I know in a new way how very much He loves me. For the rest of my life I want to serve this God Who saved me. He saved me both from eternal destruction when I received Jesus as my Lord and Savior many years ago and from death beneath the feet of an angry elephant there on the Marsibit road.

Diida's wife, Esther, is glad he wasn't trampled by the elephant.

PRAYER

Lord, nothing takes You by surprise! Thank You that You protect us and will allow only what has first passed through Your hands to affect us.

TO MEDITATE ON

His faithful promises are your armor and protection. (Psalm 91:4c, NLT)

"For I know the plans I have for you," declares the LORD, "plans to prosper you and not to harm you, plans to give you hope and a future." (Jeremiah 29:11)

TO ASK MYSELF

Do I remember to thank God each day for His protection? Do I believe that God really does have a plan for my life?

28.

"God Isn't Fair!"

 I am determined that Thou shalt be above all....Rise, O Lord, into Thy proper place of honour, above my ambitions, above my likes and dislikes, *above my family*, my health, and even life itself. Let me decrease that Thou mayest increase....
—A. W. Tozer (emphasis mine)

AFTER FOUR YEARS in Kenya supervising translation and literacy teams, we returned to the USA in late 1991 via the circuitous route of Papua New Guinea (PNG). Michael, Treesa, and 21-month-old Alyssa came from the Philippines and joined us there for Christmas. Though Treesa had not seen her dad for over four years and Alyssa had yet to meet *Babu* (Swahili for grandpa), this was not just a family reunion. We spent ten days in Mobuta village living in Pastor Panuyaba's thatch-roofed, bamboo-walled house.

After the publication of the Awa New Testament in 1974, we had visited the Awas about once a year. Now it had been almost seven years since we'd visited them.

We gathered in the church building, carpeted wall-to-wall with people. The loud singing was accompanied by guitars and homemade drums, both played with more gusto than skill. A holy hush fell as people worshiped the Lord, hands lifted and faces turned upward.

Pastor Panuyaba and Honey-Old-Man (Ed) wended their way to the pulpit. "Many years ago, when I was a teenager, this man came," the pastor began. His voice broke and his face contorted. Regaining control, he wiped his eyes. "He came and...." His voice dropped to a whisper. "He brought me Jesus. If he had not come, I would be in the 'place of fire' today. He came and brought me my Lord."

The days were filled with church-sponsored activities. Group Scripture reading was revived. Dirty, worn New Testaments told us that people had been reading, but we noted it was the older people who read.

The stock of New Testaments was almost gone. The Awas had not taught their children—many now nearing adulthood—to read in their language. Pidgin and the smattering of English that these young people knew were inadequate to communicate more than narrative Bible stories. If the church was to grow, to feed on the meat of the Word, we had to return to Awaland and help the people revise and get the New Testament reprinted and to help them train literacy supervisors. Those supervisors would then train teachers who would teach the children and the nonliterate adults to read in the language that speaks to their hearts—Awa.

We returned in January 1994. Once again, we left children and grandchildren. But that year God allowed us to see all our grandchildren. Treesa with Kendra came to PNG midyear for four weeks. Karen with her two boys stopped by the Philippines and picked up Treesa's oldest daughter before coming on to PNG in December. After Karen left...well, that's the story of—

"God Isn't Fair!"

"It's not fair!" was an oft-heard phrase in our home when our two daughters were growing up.

"Today at school Mr. Harder...," Karen would begin. A woeful tale of some supposed injustice would follow, ending with "It's not fair!"

Or Treesa might lament, "It's not fair that I *always* have to wash the dishes alone. Why can't Karen help?" On and on, week after week, it went—an all too familiar story to parents.

"You know what?" I'd reply to the plaintive it's-not-fair cry. "Life isn't fair. It's not fair that you should have a daddy and mommy who love you. Many children are unwanted and unloved; many are treated cruelly.

"You were born in a country where there's no fighting. Many kids go to bed to the sound of bombs bursting around them night after night. They know nothing but war. That's not fair.

"And it's not fair that you have plenty of food. All over the world lots of children don't know what it would feel like to have full tummies. No, life isn't fair. Sometimes it even seems that God isn't fair."

Recently I discovered the ugly it's-not-fair attitude lurking in my own heart.

The month before, Karen had brought her two sons to visit us in PNG. En route she stopped in the Philippines, where Treesa and her husband teach at Faith Academy, a school for MKs. There she picked up our four-year-old granddaughter and brought her along, too. What a glorious, though tiring, three weeks we enjoyed with our wonderful grandchildren Ricky, Michael, and Alyssa. Then they left.

Now my house, heart, and arms felt empty. Silence echoed through each room of my now too big house. My heart felt squeezed into a tiny, hard ball. My arms ached both figuratively and literally. Grandchildren-play is fun but hard on grandma-muscles. But grandchildren-absence is even more difficult!

"It's not fair!" was right on the tip of my torn emotions, seeking to express it out loud. *But of course, I'm too old to say that!* Or at least anywhere but in the shower, where only God could hear.

I was tempted to remind the Lord that many grandmothers can zip across town to spend an hour, a day, or a night with their grandchildren. My grandsons live half a world away. And although Alyssa and Kendra are only a fourth of a world away, airfare from PNG to the Philippines is expensive. Some grandmas can pick up the phone and for a few cents chat with their grandkids. But phone calls from PNG to the USA and the Philippines are budget breaking.

But why remind the Lord of all that? He already knows it. So I cried as a hot shower relaxed my aching muscles but failed to relax my cold, complaining heart.

It was almost Christmas, the time of "Joy to the World." How could I get over the it's-not-fair self-pity syndrome that was sapping not only my joy but also my energy?

Christmas. Yes, that's it. When God gave His beloved Son that first Christmas, He was operating on love, not fairness. Love for you and for me. No, Christmas isn't "fair"; John 3:16 isn't "fair."

It's not "fair" that God should love me, an undeserving sinner. But, oh, how I thank my gracious Father that He "so loved the world" (John 3:16). That includes me! It isn't fair that God was separated from Jesus, His beloved Son. Jesus left His Father to die for my sins. I praise God that because He loved "he gave his one and only Son...." But it wasn't a matter of being fair. Not at all.

It's not fair that I should be born into a kingdom of peace. But thank You, God, that the angel's announcement of "Peace on earth" included my heart and life. Thank You that John 3:16 assures me that whoever believes in Him has eternal life.

It's not fair that I should be able to feast on God's Word, served up in a language I understand. As I used to tell Karen and Treesa, "Lots of kids in this world are hungry." And they're hungry for more than food. Many of God's children hunger for His Word in their own language. They have never read in their heart-language that "God so loved the world that he gave his one and only Son, that whoever believes in him should not perish but have eternal life."

That's why this long-distance grandma has spent so many years in PNG as a Bible translator.

It's Christmas Eve now. Earlier, as I reflected on God's love, a hot shower washed away more than my early-morning garden grime; my grandma-grief went, too. I felt those ubiquitous words, "It's not fair!" recede from the tip of my tongue as the muscles of my heart relaxed in the warmth of His love—a love that always carries us to victory in an unfair world.

PRAYER

Father God, thank You that You operated not on "fairness" but on love when You sent Your Son to die for our sins! Thank You that You are a loving, just God!

TO MEDITATE ON

This is love: not that we loved God, but that He loved us and sent his Son as an atoning sacrifice for our sins. (1 John 4:10)

TO ASK MYSELF

What thoughts of self-pity are lurking in my mind and heart that are causing me to feel that God is not "fair" to me?

29.

Some Things I've Learned from Some Very GRAND Kids

 Talk and play with children. It
will bring out the unhurried
little person inside you.
—Linus Mundy

LINDA CHAIKIN IN HER NOVEL *Kingscote*[1] talks about "the merry voices
of [Burmese] children [that] filled the sultry air."

Though none of our coworkers in Papua New Guinea were from
Burma, people from over a dozen different countries work together
there in Bible translation.[2]

What cheer kids from any culture bring to our hearts. When we
take time to listen to them, we find that they say some of the most
unexpected things! And we not only laugh with them but also learn
things we never expected to learn from those "most unexpected
things." As Dale Evans says in *Grandparents Can*, "We love to repeat
the funny things [children say], because they lighten our hearts...."
Here I repeat a few of those "funny things" and note—

Some Things I've Learned
from Some Very GRAND Kids

Mark and Narda Bradshaw, Wycliffe members from Australia, served four years in Kenya, East Africa, as support workers. Their daughter made friends with Kenyan children living in the same compound. Sarah, showing a photo of herself with two of her Kenyan friends, pointed out, "I'm the one in the middle with the yellow T-shirt on."

Isn't it wonderful how "colorblind" children can be! Don't you envy them?

I've learned that...children like Tricia and Sylvia (called "the vanilla-chocolate sisters" by their mothers) can indeed be very colorblind if we allow them to be!

Three-year-old Ricky was to be baptized on Sunday, and his father felt he ought to explain what was going to happen.

"Ricky, the pastor will put some water on your head and then...," his father began.

"I don't *want* water on my head!" Ricky interrupted.

His father fixed Ricky with a stern look. "Young man," he replied, "you don't have a choice."

Ricky sat quietly for a few seconds taking in what he had just been told. "Daddy, I *choose* to have water on my head!" he announced.

I learned from my three-year-old grandson that no matter how young or old we are, we can always exercise our freedom of choice. We can *choose* to accept those things in our lives over which we have no control.

Marty Paul, a professional counselor, and his wife, Lois, who practices the gift of hospitality, travel from the USA to various countries to minister to Wycliffe people. After one trip overseas, Lois appeared in church wearing a new baby-blue sweater. Her five-year-old granddaughter Hannah noticed the new sweater as she walked down the aisle with her grandmother. "You know," she proclaimed in her not too soft, "outside" voice, "old ladies *can* look good." Hannah had observed something else about her grandmother. "And, Grandma," she added, "you don't have wrinkles on your toes."

I've learned how very, very observant kids can be!

"Where is your daddy, Bibi?" my five-year-old grandson Michael asked. Knowing that he really meant "husband," I explained that his babu (grandfather) was my husband "just as your daddy is your mommy's husband."

"Oh!" was his astute reply to that bit of sociology. "Well, then," he wanted to know, "where is your *real* daddy?"

"My daddy is with Jesus, Michael."

Again an astute, "Oh!" followed quickly by, "What you mean is, he's dead."

Well, so much for euphemisms. I learned from Michael that sometimes we adults just have to admit, along with a little child, that "the emperor doesn't have anything on!"

Yu and Kie Fukunaga, a couple from Japan, came to Papua New Guinea to teach at Ukarumpa International High School. Kazuki, their three-year-old daughter, sings a Japanese song about a dog and a cat. The dog barks *"Wan! Wan!"* and the cat meows *"Nyan! Nyan!"* in Japanese.

While Yu and Kie are busy teaching Japanese to the students from their country, Kazuki is busy learning English at preschool. One day she said to her mother, "Look at that dog. He barks, 'Woof! Woof!'"

"Yes, in Japanese, dogs bark '*Wan! Wan!*'" her mother said.

"Oh, but that dog is an American!" Kazuki noted.

Yes, children are observant! I've learned I need to watch what language I use around children, for I am representing not just America, but Heaven, to them!

Rob and June Head, Australian members, work in Papua New Guinea. They are about to see the third New Testament, which they've helped translate, go to press.

The Heads have children and grandchildren who like to talk to them occasionally by phone. One day June answered the phone and heard squeals of delight followed by their two-year-old granddaughter's shout, "Talk Ma-ma! Talk Dad-dad!"

Emily had climbed onto the stool by the phone, picked up the handset, pressed the pre-programmed button, and called Grandma and Granddad all the way from Australia.

I've learned that kids learn what technical things—like computers and these new-fang-dangled telephones—can do much faster than some of us older ones!

I've learned that...kids do take to new fang-dangled things easily!

"Alyssa, you are to pick up all your toys," our daughter Treesa told her five-year-old.

Alyssa protested, as five-year-olds will. Her mother countered her protests, as mothers of five-year-olds will. Alyssa protested again, as five-year-olds will.

Mothers of five-year-olds, however, have a frustration limit. "Alyssa!" her mother spoke firmly. "I don't intend to argue with you!"

"Well," Alyssa noted, "you already are!"

I've learned (and Treesa probably also has learned) how easy it is to get pulled into an argument, especially with a five-year-old.

Soren and Britten Ärsjo, translators in PNG from Switzerland, have grandchildren in Canada. Daughter Laila went to high school with Kevin, son of translators Marshall and Helen Lawrence. Later Kevin and Laila married.

Laila wrote that Daddy Kevin promised Kelsey and Letitia candy if they finished the food on their plates. Kelsey dawdled.

"Kelsey, you're not getting candy if you don't eat. You're in for a rude surprise!" Laila warned.

More dawdling. Finally, Kelsey pushed her almost untouched plate toward her mother and said in a pleading voice, "Mommy, can I have my rude surprise *now*, please!"

I've learned that children will hold you to your promise, so it's best to be careful what you promise!

Older brothers were helping Mom, busy cooking supper for the visiting pastor and his wife, by bathing younger brother. All went well until three-year-old Marshall escaped from the bathroom. He sauntered into the living room, clothed only in a smile. He headed for the couch and squeezed himself in between the astounded company. Nobody seemed to know what to say. Nobody, that is, except Marshall. He looked up at the pastor, then looked down at his feet. "Heh, heh, heh," he giggled. "I'm barefooted."

Like my nephew Marshall, I've learned that sometimes it's just as well to focus on the more insignificant things of life!

Chewing gum! How the Awa kids loved it. They would scour the hillsides for wild strawberries or go up into the forest for tree tomatoes. Either was a fair trade for a piece of the coveted "food that you don't swallow but just keep chewing and chewing."

"*Aneq nahno?* [What are you eating?]" five-year-old Maemaka asked me one day.

"*Arore* [A-row-ray—from the word *lollie*]," I answered as I opened my mouth to show him.

The next thing I knew, my gum had been snatched from between my teeth and was in Maemaka's mouth! Maemaka obviously thought ABC (already been chewed) gum was better than no gum!

I learned that day that sometimes we have to snatch the opportunity at hand, or in this case, from the mouth!

Arjen Lock, from the Netherlands, and his wife, Maiya, from Finland, are Bible translators in PNG. When their son, Werner, was five years old, he spoke Dutch to his father and Finnish to his mother. In the village where they lived, he spoke to the adults in their Abau language. And when Werner played with the village children, he talked to them in Pidgin English.

We were in the Locks' village home for an administrative visit. In clear though slightly clipped English, Werner asked us, "Uncle and Auntie, do you want to hear a story?" Yes, we certainly did want to hear this charming multilingual child's story. "One day I was following a pig down the path. He *excreted* on the path right in front of me!"

Obviously no one had told Werner that the "correct" way for a five-year-old to talk about that function in English was to say, "went potty."

I have learned that children have wonderful, receptive minds. They *can* assimilate more than one language at a time if given the opportunity!

"Treesa is swearing! You must beat her!" Awa adults would tattle on our youngest daughter, only three years old at the time.

"What did she say?"[3]

The answer was always the same: "Oh, it's too bad to repeat."

"Well, Treesa doesn't swear in English. Only in Awa. *You* taught her to swear. And you also teach *your children* to swear."

An Awa always vehemently denied that charge. "Well, how did Treesa and your children learn to swear?" I would ask.

"Well, ahhhhh...they...aaaa...they just do it."

One day in the village, Treesa was playing with her kitty right outside an open window. Holding compliant Kitty by the neck, she spanked him and accused him of being "a bad kitty." Then to reinforce that she told him, "*Awahpete ání móne!*"[4]

That phrase said by one Awa woman to another Awa woman shows camaraderie.[5] But if a woman says it to her husband, she might find herself hit over the head with the blunt end of an ax! (Her husband wouldn't *really* want to kill her, just teach her a little lesson.)

Translated into English, that phrase did not have the emotive content to me as it did to the Awa. So I didn't "beat" my three-year-old swearer. I just tried to communicate that there were more appropriate phrases to use when her pet was "a bad kitty."

I've learned that...big people can all too easily teach little people bad habits. (No, Ryan isn't smoking a cigar. He has one of his grandmother's curlers in his mouth.)

I learned long ago that it's a good thing to do as the old Sunday school song says, "Be careful little lips what you say!" Little ears do listen, and little lips do repeat.

Steve and Holly Hong, Korean-Americans, are Bible translators. They live in a hot, humid part of Papua New Guinea, an almost perfect place for kids to go barefooted.

Friends from the USA visited the Hongs in the village where they live and work. "Joohyun," one of them said to the Hongs' five-year-old daughter, "you'll have to wear shoes when you come to America."

"Why?" Joohyun responded incredulously. "Are there lots of pig droppings on the paths there, too?"

Communication, I've learned, is indeed a complex process. A lot of implied information gets communicated as wrong information if we're not careful.

Nelly, a young Filipina, came to visit Treesa. After she had left, Treesa prayed with Alyssa and Kendra that God would send Nelly a godly husband. Kendra mulled over that and concluded that "It *is* important to marry a man who loves Jesus. If he didn't love Jesus, he might do bad things to you. He might stick out his tongue at you."

I've learned that...when life's problems cause me to feel "up in the air," a loving Father is always there for me.

I've learned that my grandchildren have no idea of what cruel things a man *can* do to his wife. And I praise God for my wonderful sons-in-law!

Three-year-old Matthias came home from preschool in PNG and proudly showed off his handicraft to Papi (his Swiss father) and Mama (his German mother): a picture of the empty tomb. "Jesus isn't here anymore," he explained. "He's in Russia."

His translator parents, Thomas and Christiane Weber, figured out that puzzle: "Jesus is risen!" Matthias's preschool teacher had told her class. To Matthias, "risen" pronounced with a non-German accent sounds a lot like German *Russland*—Russia.

I've learned it's wise to speak slowly and clearly to children, especially where there are competing accents!

Joanne Locnikar, a Wycliffe member in Papua New Guinea, works as a literacy specialist. Also a schoolteacher, she first came to PNG as an STA[6] and taught two years at the group primary school. It was the last hour of what had seemed a long day. She began the social studies lesson: "The three things a person needs to survive." Children responded with the right answers: food, clothing, and shelter. The lesson had gone well. Now it was almost finished, and Joanne ignored a waving hand. *Don't blow this lesson for me, little girl,* she thought. *I'm tired and want to finish without any controversy.* Finally, a bit impatiently, she called on the persistent hand waver.

"Yes, what is it, Melanie?"

"Miss Locnikar, you forgot one more thing a person needs to survive."

Joanne grimaced inwardly. *Yeah, right. I've taught this lesson many times over the years, and now you're going to tell me I forgot something?* She forced herself to smile at her eager student. "And what is that?"

"We need love to survive. God's love."

What is that humbling statement: "Out of the mouths of babes..."?

Joanne says, "I discovered that I wasn't the teacher that day. Rather I was the student learning from God through a child." If we've not discovered that already, it's only because we've not been around children long enough.

PRAYER

"Lord, make me childlike. Deliver me from the urge to compete with another for place or prestige or position. I would be simple and artless as a little child. Deliver me from pose and pretense." A.W. Tozer

TO MEDITATE ON

He called a little child....And he said: "I tell you the truth, unless you change and become like little children, you will never enter the kingdom of heaven....whoever welcomes a little child like this in my name welcomes me. But if anyone causes one of these little ones who believe in me to sin, it would be better for him to have a large millstone hung around his neck and be drowned in the depths of the sea." (Matthew 18:2–3, 5–6)

TO ASK MYSELF

Am I careful what I do and say around children? What can I do where I am that will result in "the little children" coming to Jesus?

---

1. Linda Chaikin, *Kingscote*, Chapter 17, "Heart of India," p. 231.
2. Besides having over 250 people from our host country, we have coworkers from Australia, Canada, Finland, the Netherlands, the British Isles, Japan, Korea, Sweden, New Zealand, Switzerland, Germany, Austria, Singapore, Norway, and one from the island of Barbados in the Caribbean. (Information from "SIL PNG Branch Statistics," August 1997. The countries are listed in order beginning with the countries with the largest number of representatives.)

3. This and other reported conversations with Awas throughout the book took place in the Awa language.

4. The English translation: You're a child from the birth canal!

5. In the same way, American men use "S.O.B." to show camaraderie.

6. STA stands for short-term assistant, but we jokingly say it really means sure to apply!

30.

A Redeemed Symbol

 The widow—she offered her mite.
Oh, how precious it was in God's sight!
Only a little boy with fish. His offering
Caused heaven's angels to dance-'n-sing.
Offer Him your all! Be it new or old,
He will redeem it, turn it to gold!
—Aretta Loving

AUNAH, ETARO, AND MARENÚ. At the dedication of the revised Awa New Testament how proud we were of these three Awa men. And how grateful to God for the Mattockses, the van Dorens, and many other support workers, too numerous to mention here. Let me tell you first about these two support couples, then a word about the three Awa men.

In early 1994, we returned to PNG at the invitation of Awa Christians to help them revise the almost out of print New Testament. Well-used copies were dirty, worn, and tattered. In the four years we worked with the Awas on the revision, Rich and Joyce Mattocks, a couple of great people from Washington state, acted as our support link with Ukarumpa. "Rich," we'd say on our two-way radio, "we heard on the morning flight sked that the helicopter will be in our area next week doing work for New Tribes missionaries. Alan says he can stop by here. Would you or Joyce phone the post office and ask them to send our mail to the hangar? Also please check at the store to see if they have flea powder. And a packet of dried beans and...."

Despite their being busy teachers at the primary school, Rich and Joyce always cheerfully did whatever we asked.

I met Rich in our group-run store the first week we came back to PNG to work with the Awas in New Testament revision and literacy. When I introduced myself, Rich announced, "We've been praying for you in the highlands prayer meeting! If you don't have a support team yet, Joyce and I would like to be your team." That really made me take notice of this young man. Not that he's hard to notice: over six feet tall, with dark, wavy hair—and he limps. "My limp is the result of my wrestling match with an angel over going to the mission field," Rich jokes.

Ed and the literary supervisors (with family) rejoice
at the dedication of the revised Awa New Testament.

And what a joke! Rich felt that God wanted him to serve overseas as a special education teacher, and he wanted a wife to go with him. Rich's brother-in-law, one of Joyce's Bible school professors, had talked Joyce into going on a blind date with Rich to "talk about missions."

It was only after Joyce had agreed that he told her that Rich had cerebral palsy. *Oh, no!* Joyce thought. *What have I gotten myself in for!* But being a trooper, she didn't back out, and that date led the couple to the marriage altar!

It soon becomes apparent to anyone who knows Rich that his congenital handicap is not a great deterrent to him. Rich and Joyce visited us for a week in Awaland. Acting like a kid himself, he taught the Awa kids to blow soap bubbles. He climbed up and down those mountain trails almost as though he'd been born there.

Prior to the revised Awa New Testament dedication, three-month-old Christa probably felt somewhat neglected by a usually very attentive father. Rich spent a lot of his evening hours arranging bookings for support people to fly out to the celebration.

Alan van Doren, a JAARS pilot from New Jersey, was a former police helicopter pilot. When he and his wife, Debbie, heard that Wycliffe could use helicopter pilots to fly translators into hard-to-get-to places, Alan exchanged a career that provided lots of excitement and secure benefits for one that offered a different kind of excitement—and benefits that are "out of this world!" On dedication day, Alan ferried five loads of people out to celebrate with us and the Awas. Debbie and their latest little "van," five-month-old Trevor, were among the guests!

As the ceremony proceeded, we rejoiced to see Aunah, Etaro, and Marenú in action. These three men were chosen by their people to train at Ukarumpa to become literacy supervisors among their people. Ed mentored them over a period of two years at five different courses held at Ukarumpa and during their practicum in the village. Two young Australian men, Glenn McIntosh and Rodney Grace, came to PNG with "Venture 24," a two-year hands-on literacy training course sponsored by Wycliffe Australia. They helped mentor the Awa men for about twelve months.

At the dedication, we saw that Aunah, Etaro, and Marenú not only had become adept literacy supervisors but also had become adept planners. The program they directed involved many Awa villagers,

young and old. Music, a sermon, skits. Ed and I were honored by a
speech chronicling our history of involvement with the Awas. We
were given gifts: string bags, pig tusk necklaces, beautifully decorated
arrows. Our hearts rejoiced as one skit portrayed our early days among
the Awa. In that skit I saw—

A Redeemed Symbol

It was 1960.

"*Anerono,* [What are you doing?]" I ask a mother rubbing slimy
red mud on her child's body.

"I'm rubbing mud on my son," she answers.

That was obvious. I should have asked, "Anesabebo. [Why?]"

"So his father won't beat him."

I stand and watch as she continues to rub mud on every part of his
body. *Why*, I wonder, *would the father want to beat his little son?* Then I
remember. *His father?! He died in a flu epidemic before we came. At the
anniversary of his death, his wahnsa {ghost}, she believes, will be wandering
around the village. Now their child is particularly vulnerable to the wrath of
his father's wahnsa. The red mud will protect her son so the wahnsa will not
be able to beat him and make him ill.*

How sad I feel that I don't yet know Awa well enough to tell this
mother that the blood of Jesus, not red mud, can protect from evil
spirits!

Thirty-seven years later—

At the 1997 dedication of the revised Awa New Testament, two
teenagers painted their faces with red mud. In a skit they portrayed
Órétah-Korení (that's me: Aretta-Old-Woman) and Ani-Kore (that's
Ed: Honey-Old-Man). The teenagers, dressed in clothes, walked
among people wearing bark skirts and bark capes. The people also wore
pig tusks through their noses and were crowned with cassowary-feather
head dressings. We were the "red ones" (as they've always called us).

We came. By God's grace we brought His Word. The people now know what we came to tell them: that the blood of Jesus, not red mud, protects them from evil spirits!

Red mud. Once a symbol of death, mourning, fear of retaliation from the *wahnsa*—the ghosts, the spirits—now a symbol of life and rejoicing, freedom from fear of the spirits! Red mud—a redeemed symbol!

PRAYER

Father, thank You that we have Your Word in our language. Give us the concern and compassion that will lead us to do something about those who are not as blessed as we are, for those who have not heard that Jesus died and that His blood protects us from the evil one.

TO MEDITATE ON

You were redeemed from the empty way of life handed down to you from your forefathers...with the precious blood of Christ, a lamb without blemish or defect. (1 Peter 1:18–19)

They overcame him by the blood of the Lamb and by the word of their testimony. (Revelation 12:11a)

TO ASK MYSELF

What old practices in my life will I allow God to redeem and use for His glory?

EPILOGUE

Like Noisy Children

 Children can be such joyful additions to our so often serious and stuffy world. They open our eyes to the wonders of creation and make us consider such important questions as, "How do the stars stay in the sky?" and "Why is the grass green instead of red?"
—Corrie ten Boom

THE AWA NEW TESTAMENT has been revised and reprinted! It was dedicated in a glorious celebration ceremony in Mobuta village in late October 1997. Believers and others who are "on the way" are reading it. Ed and I left PNG a short time after the dedication.

"Why did you leave so soon?" we've been asked. Awas were trained to do the work that needs to be done among their people, and to do it in a culturally appropriate way. Had we remained, the Awas would have looked to us for direction, help, and support. Our desire is that the Christian leaders and literacy supervisors look to God, not to us, to meet those needs. Only as they do so will His work among them be truly indigenous (that is, self-governing, self-supporting, self-propagating, and self-expressing) and continue to grow strong.

On the way home, we stopped in the Philippines, where we welcomed Andrew Michael Hause, our sixth grandchild, into this world.

A national church that is "self-expressing" will look to God, not to the missionary.

Now we are living near the JAARS[1] center. Karen and Lyle, with their three sons, live only about an hour away. Since they both are active in their church, we often have the joy of our three noisy, rambunctious grandsons being "dumped" on us for a weekend!

One of these years we hope to spend a few months in the Philippines working in a support role. We look forward to having our grandchildren there "dumped" on us some weekends while their parents get away alone!

Life in North Carolina is different from life overseas. But one thing that has not changed is our enjoyment of birds, God's varied and manifold creation.

In PNG we reveled in seeing the mischievous white cockatoo that sometimes pulled clothespins off the line, dumping clothes in the mud; the hornbill, appearing so diffident; the green bird (which acted somewhat like an American quail) that came with his mate to eat grass seeds right outside our bedroom door in the village; the small sunbirds that lit on the tall, thin grass reeds for the thrill of a seesaw ride; and last, but by no means least, the resplendent, illusive birds of paradise (the actual bird, not the flower of the same name). The *greater bird of paradise* with its dense mass of plumes holds the honor of being the national emblem on Papua New Guinea's coat of arms.

In Kenya, the brilliant yellow weaverbird came to eat seed from our second-story apartment deck. When driving through the savanna, we would slow down and watch as gaggles of guinea fowls leisurely crossed the road. Unlike the guinea fowls, the stately crowned crane and the strange-looking, black-pantalooned secretary bird, both over a yard tall, merely stood in the nearby savanna and gawked back at us. The largest bird in the world, the male African ostrich may grow to a height of eight feet and weigh as much as three hundred pounds! We often saw these flightless birds in the game park near Nairobi exercising their gift of speed: They are able to exceed fifty miles an hour! Like all tourists, we took a safari to Lake Navasha to see the hundreds and hundreds of pink flamingo, many of which stood in the water perfectly balanced on one spindly leg.

Here in North Carolina, from our deck we watch the red-headed woodpecker, the brilliant cardinal, the hummingbird drinking sugar-water from our feeder. The flashy blue jay calls to us, "Do it! Do it!" That reminds us that there is training and teaching of new members for us to do, and we're grateful that we can "do it!"

Just as the birds of PNG and Kenya, the birds in North Carolina are—

Like Noisy Children

They come.
And like noisy children
They flit here and there.

And like children they squabble.
Some get their feathers ruffled.
Like finicky eaters
They peck away at their food.

But their noise is chirpy, happy birdsong:
"There's food and water on this window ledge.
A Heavenly Father surely knows our needs!"
They sing their song of thanks to God alone!
Lord, let me see my children's noise
As happy, exuberant sounds of youth
And enjoy their noise as I
Enjoy these birds at my window.

Let me bear with their squabbles
Knowing that when I ignore them,
They themselves will eventually
Smooth "the ruffled feathers."

And when they pick and peck at their food,
Let me remember that You made them children,
Not adults who eat spinach and Brussels sprouts
Without a blink of the eye.

And most of all, Lord,
Let me enjoy them *now*
As much as I enjoyed
My feathered friends this morning.

For like those birds they come into my view
For a short time only.
Then they fly away,
"Leave the nest," they say.

And I'm left aching, wishing I could
Hear again the noise,
See again "the ruffled feathers,"
Cook again food they would peck away at...

"Oh, Honey! Listen to that noise!"
"The birds you mean?"
"No, she's bringing the grandkids
To visit us today!"

Neither Ed nor I am what you'd call serious, gung-ho bird watch-ers. That is, we don't rise before dawn, hang binoculars around our necks, and tramp into the forest, then lie silently on the damp ground for hours at a time waiting for a certain bird to make its appearance. But we have enjoyed the birds we've "known," and we have noticed they really can act a lot like noisy children. We ask ourselves why we didn't take time to enjoy our two noisy, squabbling daughters even more when they were growing up.

One of our goals now that we're living in the States is to see more of our three full-of-energy grandsons who live only an hour's drive from us! Together we'll play games, go on hikes, watch TV—football and basketball games, the Rose Parade. We'll read to them. Ed has already begun to teach them to shoot a BB gun and to use an ax and a machete.

But we'll probably look back in a few years and ask ourselves again why didn't we take even more time to enjoy them? The answer to that question and to the former one concerning our daughters is the same: There are people out there who have never read, some have never even heard, John 3:16 in their own language. So we'll be continuing in the work of Bible translation. Not actually translating another New Testament. We'll serve on Quest[2] staff in California and ICC[3] staff here at the JAARS Center in North Carolina. We'll continue to be part of a team. A team that helps train younger folk who will translate or facilitate nationals (like Zaccheaus) to translate God's Word; also those who will work in literacy or work alongside nationals (like Diida); and those who will support those translators and literacy workers: teachers (like the Mattockses) or pilots (like Alan van Doren) or—Well, I reiterate what Uncle Cam said, "We can use anyone in the task of Bible translation except a bartender. And we could even use him if he got converted!"

So, as they say in Southern USA, "Y'all come!" Yes, come join us. Come and use your talents and skills in Bible translation. Come and be part of a team that is bringing God's Word to those who have never heard!

PRAYER

Children, whether my own or those of a close friend or relative, are indeed a blessing from You, O Lord! Give us wisdom as You allow us for oh, such a short time, to train them and to guide them into Your paths.

TO MEDITATE ON

When you see the children that I...give you, then you will acknowledge that I am the holy God.... (Isaiah 29:23 TEV)

And the things you have heard me say in the presence of many witnesses entrust to reliable men who will also be qualified to teach others. (2 Timothy 2:2)

TO ASK MYSELF

Do I fret and moil over "noisy children" (my own or those in the neighborhood, at church or wherever)? Or am I able to relax and enjoy children?

---

1. See Appendix F.
2. See Appendix I.
3. See Appendix J.

Appendix A

On April 23, 1982, William Cameron Townsend died at the age of eighty-five. His gravesite is at the JAARS Center on Davis Road in Waxhaw, North Carolina, between the Mexico-Cardenas Museum and the Museum of the Alphabet. He was the founder of the Summer Institute of Linguistics (now known as SIL International) and Wycliffe Bible Translators (WBT), the sister organization of SIL International. This giant of a man was affectionately known to many simply as "Uncle Cam." Uncle Cam's widow, Elaine Townsend, lives near the JAARS Center and still takes an active part in speaking on behalf of WBT and JAARS.

Appendix B

SIL International
International Linguistics Center (ILC)
7500 W. Camp Wisdom Road
Dallas, TX 75236-5699, USA
PHONE: 972-708-7400
FAX: 972-708-7433
WEB SITE: www.sil.org

The *Ethnologue* brings together up-to-date information available on every known language in the world. SIL International publishes a new edition every four years and makes it available on the Internet. Over 6,700 languages are listed in the *Ethnologue*. Of those, there are still over 2,000 whose speakers do not have even a part of the Bible. These languages are usually unwritten or, if written, are often unanalyzed. To learn one of these languages behind the "language curtain" demands the best that the young missionary volunteer has to offer. Basic preparation is essential. SIL offers the training needed for that task.

SIL began primarily as one man's compassion and concern for people in smaller language groups. In 1919, William Cameron Townsend, without formal linguistic training, worked cross-culturally with the Mayan Cakchiquel people of Guatemala. Despite his lack of training, he made a significant contribution to linguistic, education, and translation work among the Cakchiquel people.

By 1929 his concern had broadened to include other people groups. His pioneering work became the foundation for the first training sessions for others who would follow his path. These summer courses began on a farm in the state of Arkansas in 1934 with three students.

In 1935 Uncle Cam, as he became known to his followers, led a small group of young people into Mexico to study its many Amerindian languages. Kenneth L. Pike was among that group. He began work on the Mixteco language in a remote village in the state of Oaxaca. Through the years he spent much of his time helping other SIL people with their work, particularly on the study of tone. He also translated the New Testament for the Mixteco. Today Dr. Pike is internationally known as one of the world's leading linguistics.

Those who joined SIL and WBT in the 1940s and 1950s began using their SIL training by working in much of the Americas. Their basic approach, like that of the founder, revolved around village life: language and culture learning; studying the structure (the grammar) of the language; developing an alphabet; constructing primers, readers on health, geography, science, and other educational topics; making a diglot dictionary; and translating the Bible or portions of the Bible. Research was done under the sponsorship of national government agencies. SIL workers always made the written results of their research available to others.

After SIL established work in the Americas, in 1952 Dr. Richard Pittman spearheaded the same work in the Philippines. From there it spread to other parts of the Pacific and Asia, to Africa in 1962, and to parts of Europe in 1974.

Today SIL, an international educational organization, specializes in the scientific study of vernacular languages in dozens of countries. Members of SIL International share a Christian commitment to serve language communities worldwide through a strategy that integrates translation, literacy, and language-based development. One way SIL keeps that commitment is by offering courses in linguistics and literacy. Summer courses are offered in linguistics at two universities in the United States. Courses are also offered in New Zealand, England, France, Germany, and at two sites in Australia. One, the Asia SIL, draws students from Korea, Singapore, Japan, and other Asian countries.

Today, many thousands of people serving with more than forty mission boards on every continent of the world have taken one or more of these SIL courses. Students, missionaries on furlough, and those seeking to translate for unwritten languages comprise those "many thousands of people."

The Graduate Institute of Applied Linguistics (GIAL), a two-year postgraduate course, is closely affiliated with SIL International. It is located on the ILC's campus in Dallas. GIAL offers an MA degree in Applied Linguistics or in Language Development. GIAL faculty bring a wide range of field experience to the classroom, in addition to expertise acquired through advanced studies.

SIL International works in cooperation with universities, host governments, and private agencies in over sixty countries of the world.

Pioneer translators are serving minority language groups through linguistics, literacy, Bible translation, and many other practical services.

Forty years ago, a book titled *Two Thousand Tongues to Go* was written chronicling the story of Wycliffe Bible Translators. The title reflected what people then believed was the number of languages still needing a translation of God's Word. Since that time, language surveys have identified many more languages—more than Uncle Cam ever dreamed existed. So, today that number has not changed. In fact, the number of languages that still need a translation of God's Word may be closer to 3,000 than to 2,000. With that knowledge in mind, at a recent international conference, SIL adopted a resolution called *Vision 2025*. In part, that resolution reads: "Motivated by the pressing need for all peoples to have access to the Word of God in a language that speaks to their hearts, and reaffirming our historic values and our trust in God to accomplish the impossible, we embrace the vision that by the year 2025 a Bible translation project will be in progress for every people group that needs it....We commit ourselves to pray for the fulfillment of this vision, seeking God's guidance and obeying Him in whatever new directions He may lead."

Wycliffe Bible Translators (WTB)
P.O. Box 628200
Orlando, FL 32862-8200, USA
PHONE: 407-852-3600
                 800-Wycliff (992-5433)
FAX: 407-852-3601
EM: info_usa@wycliffe.org
WEB SITE: www.wycliffe.org

Wycliffe Bible Translators, the sister organization of SIL International, came into existence, about the same time or soon after SIL came into existence. Uncle Cam wisely realized that workers would need a representative body to look after their finances and to recruit more workers to join them.

And that is what Wycliffe Bible Translators does—that and more.

WBT is named after John Wycliffe. Wycliffe and his followers first translated the Bible into English in the fourteenth century. Today with a membership approaching six thousand, WBT's goal is to see the Bible become available to people of every group in *their* mother tongue.

WBT is the organization that recruits translators and support personnel for the work. Wycliffe is constantly seeking laborers to move into new areas.

A second major area of responsibility is "member care." When members from overseas come home for furlough, they are well looked after by competent home-assigned people or sometimes Wycliffe members on extended furlough.

Another work that Wycliffe is responsible for is fund raising, primarily for "special projects": everything from airplanes to a new children's home. (All Wycliffe members, whether translators or support personnel, are responsible for their own financial support. They look to God to supply their needs through churches, friends, and relatives who are interested in the work of Bible translation.)

A fourth area of responsibility that falls under Wycliffe's domain is relating and communicating to the home constituency, that is, to those people who support the work of Bible translation throughout the world by prayer and finance. Closely related to that is the area of interfacing with the churches that send out workers and are in partnership with those workers through giving and praying.

Over all these five areas of responsibility is the covering of prayer which Wycliffe Bible Translators takes very seriously. One Wycliffe brochure reads, "We continue to make our requests known, trusting God for His leading and His provision in all areas of the work," and "WYCLIFFE WANTS TO HELP YOU PRAY with knowledge and understanding." To do the latter, Wycliffe publishes *The Intercessor,* a one-page newsletter, a publication that provides up-to-date information, requests and answers to prayers, focusing on different aspects of the work and other corporate needs. *Up Close,* a one-page, quarterly publication, provides day by day, personal prayer requests from WBT workers and their families around the world.

The Bibleless Peoples Prayer Project links people with a language group yet to be reached. Those who sign up are assigned a group and information and updates about the group are sent to them. George Cowan, founder of this prayer project, says, "Nothing will give prayer priority and encourage faithfulness in prayer more than considering it an appointment with Christ Himself. He has promised to be there."

Appendix C

Because of the mountainous terrain of the highlands of Papua New Guinea, one author wrote, "God must have made New Guinea on Saturday night and dumped in all the leftovers."

Rosalie M. Donais's picturesque description in *To Them Gave He Power*[*] reads: "The highlands are a magnificently convoluted terrain, densely upholstered with rain forest. Silvery limestone crags catch the sunlight amid an incredible array of greens. Pink, gold, crimson, and purple flowers accent the forest. Half the acreage is virgin, growing half the world's plant families. Banana trees with huge vinyl leaves, samo trees looking like ming-tree cutouts standing at attention, casuarina trees, pandanus or ank nut palms grace the landscape. Gargantuan ferns curl out of marshy soil. Brilliant scarlet and purple coleus are as common as dandelions. Daisies, cream and red poinsettia, canna lilies, frangipani, bougainvillea and hibiscus dazzle the eye. Tiny purple orchids hide in the tangled growth.

"Tussocks of tall *kunai* grass crowd the canegrass and multiply deliriously, their pink and mauve fronds dancing on every breath of air. Groves of *pit pit* grow everywhere. The razor-sharp grass-leaves are dried and pounded, and woven into herringbone-patterned floor mats, as well as the indispensable raincapes."

---

[*] *To Them Gave He Power* is available from ACC Foundation, Inc., 1135 Sholey Road, Richmond, VA 23231. Phone: 804-222-1943; Fax: 804-236-0642.

Appendix D

The American Missionary Fellowship (AMF)
672 Conestoga Road, Box 370
Villanova, PA 19085, USA
PHONE: 610-527-4439
EM: info@americanmissionary.org
WEB SITE: www.americanmissionary.org

AMF exists to evangelize, disciple and congregate the yet unreached peoples of the United States for Jesus Christ. For over 150 years, AMF was known as the American Sunday School Union (ASSU). Under that name, missionaries pioneered the establishment of Sunday Schools which taught the Bible and brought God's plan of salvation to the country's growing frontiers. The ASSU started over 120,000 new Sunday Schools in its first one hundred years, many of which continue today as churches.

Today, AMF missionaries minister in both rural and urban settings. Church planting, Release Time classes, home Bible studies, Vacation Bible Schools, Christian camps, inner-city/cross-cultural ministries, and Sunday Schools are all part of the mission's ministry diversity. Through personal discipleship and intensive training, groups of believers are nurtured. Whenever possible, this means the establishment of a vital, mature church. AMF missionaries reach over 100,000 lives each year with the hope of eternal life in Jesus Christ.

AMF's roots go back to Glouchester, England, and Robert Raikes in the 1780s. Rev. William White, Philadelphia-born rector of Christ Church, traveled to England where he observed Raikes's Sunday Schools which had started seven years earlier. After returning to the United States, White joined forces with a nonsectarian group to start Sunday Schools which offered religious instruction to those of the lower class. With the help of Dr. Benjamin Rush (a prominent Philadelphia physician and signer of the Declaration of Independence) and William Carey (a Philadelphia book publisher who had fled Ireland to avoid persecution for writings against the government), White established the First Day

Society of Philadelphia. The Society appointed White as president, an office he held for forty-six years.

By the turn of the century, the First Day Society had given free religious education to over 2,000 students. Within twenty years, churches, which at first opposed the Sunday School movement, began to recognize Sunday Schools as an educational arm of the church. In 1817, the Philadelphia Sunday and Adult School Union was established to assist in starting Sunday Schools. It was reorganized in 1824 and called the American Sunday School Union, thus creating a national Sunday School organization.

In 1817, the mission published its first book called *Little Henry and his Bearer,* which met with such success that they published 98,000 books over the following five years. Also published were 25,000 hymnals and 500,000 "Scripture tickets." The latter could be traded in for books or gifts as a reward for Scripture memorization. Mark Twain wrote of these Scripture tickets in *The Adventures of Tom Sawyer.*

In 1821, the board of managers took a bold step and hired its first paid missionary, Rev. William Blair, a student at Princeton Seminary. In his first year, he rode by horseback from Philadelphia to North Carolina starting Sunday Schools along the way. That year, he started sixty-one new Sunday Schools, assisted fifty-five established Sunday Schools, founded six tract societies and four adult schools. After this, the board adopted the permanent policy of hiring paid full-time missionaries.

By 1824, the the Union logged 720 Sunday Schools in seventeen states with 55,000 members, making it the largest society in the USA. In 1831, the Union launched the Mississippi Valley Enterprise. The purpose of this project was to start a Sunday School in every destitute place in the Mississippi Valley. Francis Scott Key and Daniel Webster were part of this endeavor, along with hundreds of ASSU missionaries. In a few years, some 10,000 Sunday Schools were planted in midwestern settlements. More significantly, thousands were led to confess their faith in Jesus Christ. In one year alone, 17,000 people came to Christ. Even more amazingly, more than 20,000 teachers were converted during the Mississippi Valley Enterprise, according to the official mission reports.

As Americans moved west, ASSU missionaries were at their side. However, in 1861 the Civil War broke out. These were troubling days for the ASSU! Missionaries and students were on both sides of the front lines.

During the summer of 1923, ASSU pioneered the Daily Vacation Bible School (DVBS) in Minnesota. The Union also held one of the first Bible camps for young people in the early 1900s. Thus began a new phase of ministry for ASSU. VBSs, home Bible studies, and retreats soon became popular ministries.

By the 1960s, ASSU publications were being overshadowed with the fast growing denominational and independent publication houses. In 1968, the board of managers voted to phase out publications and literature.

In 1974, ASSU changed its name to the American Missionary Fellowship (AMF), a name that reflected the growing trend to use a variety of ministry methods in addition to the Sunday School. Though methods have changed over the years, the message has remained the same. Uncompromised in its biblical standards, AMF faces greater challenges today than ever before.

Today, AMF targets inner cities with the gospel of Jesus Christ where there is a compelling need to reach the multi-cultural population. Along with the inner-city ministries, many rural areas of the United States continue to be without any evangelical witness as more churches close their doors.

One hundred sixty missionary families serve with AMF in thirty-three states. These missionary families reach people of all ages and cultures in a variety of locations.

Appendix E

Viewing the collection of stick and leaf insects, beetles, and butter-flies at the Parliament House in Port Moresby, the capital of Papua New Guinea, I learned that:

- when stick and leaf insects lose legs, another leg regenerates.
- the Hermachus morosus genus "could well include the world's longest stick insect." (The displayed specimen was over 16.5 inches long.)
- the Batocera wallacel beetle, found on Breadfruit trees is "one of the longest beetles in the world." Its antennae alone may measure up to 10 inches.
- PNG is home to the largest butterfly in the world: the female Ornithoptera Birdwing found in a relatively small area around Popondetta in the Oro Province. Threatened by population pressure and the agriculture and timber industries, it has become the subject of a conservation program. The people of Oro Province are deservedly proud of being host to this birdwing butterfly. It is displayed in their provincial flag. The Oro provincial minister gives visitors to his province neckties with the Ornithoptera crafted on them.
- PNG is also home to what many regard as the most beautiful butterfly in the world. Ornithoptera Paradisea or the Paradise Birdwing, found in the North Western Province, is sought after by collectors. It, too, is a protected species.
- the Eupholus group of beetles "is the largest family of animals in the world with well over 60,000 representatives in Papua New Guinea." This group and the Rhinoscapha are commonly called the Painted Weevils.

Appendix F

JAARS
P.O. Box 248
Waxhaw, North Carolina 28173, USA
PHONE: 704-843-6000
FAX: 704-843-6200
EM: info@jaars.org
WEB SITE: www.jaars.org

As early as 1926, before the Cakchiquel New Testament was finished, Uncle Cam saw the need for airplanes and radios in SIL. His concern at the time was for those living and working in remote areas of South America. Yet it was not until 1946, when the Peruvian government invited SIL into their country, that the organization purchased its first aircraft. The military surplus Grumman Duck was used to fly translators into locations in Amazonia.

Uncle Cam also recognized the need for well-trained pilots and good equipment. The impetus needed to convince others of that need came in 1947. He and his wife, Elaine, were injured in a small commercial plane crash in Chiapas, Mexico. After that, Uncle Cam resolved to ensure the safety of translators. Although Jungle Aviation and Radio Service (now JAARS) began in Peru in 1948, operating as a small department of SIL, it was not officially incorporated until 1963.

In 1960, a Charlotte, North Carolina, businessman, Henderson Belk, donated a large tract of pine woodlands to JAARS for establishing a training and technical support center. More land has been acquired and today the center lies on 600 acres, divided by a 3,300-foot airstrip, Townsend Field. The JAARS Center is thirty miles south of Charlotte, five miles south of Waxhaw.

Many of the people groups among whom SIL International translators live and work are in extremely isolated places. Therefore they are completely dependent on air service and two-way radios.

These original two aspects of service, aviation and radio, are still a vital part of JAARS. And through the years more and more services have been added. In recognition of that diversification, the name Jungle Aviation and Radio Service (and the acronym J.A.A.R.S.) was dropped, and the organization is now called JAARS.

One vital service for today that has come into its own at the JAARS Center is computer technology and training. Using computers improves the accuracy and speeds up typesetting of Scripture. New advances make computers available to every translator no matter how remote the area where he or she lives and works.

JAARS now also serves Bible translators around the world in the areas of telecommunications, construction, maintenance, purchasing and shipping, materials transportation, and constituency and vernacular media.

The JAARS publication *Beyond*, with Kristin Holley as editor, is published six times a year. *Beyond* communicates the ministry of JAARS to a mailing list of over 25,000 people worldwide. Its purpose is to get people involved in praying, giving, and going. In 1996, this inspirational and informational magazine won two awards from the Evangelical Press Association.

Recently, a 30,000-square-foot building was constructed at the JAARS Center. It now serves as the Language Services Center (LSC). The LSC provides a facility for developing new computer and telecommunication applications for linguistics, literacy, and translation. That means that the computer department with its staff of sixty professionals, the telecommunications department, and a cadre of experienced translators researching and writing translation helps here at the JAARS Center are now housed under one roof.

These three groups (the International Computer Services, the JAARS Telecommunications Service and those translators doing research and writing helps) were scattered over the center in four buildings and three trailers. Imagine *one* building which transmits advice to several thousands of translators around the world on matters ranging from accessing language data on the computer system to removing dead ants from a laptop computer screen.

The LSC is a huge boost to efficiency and productivity—all to further the task of Bible translation worldwide, the purpose for which the JAARS Center exists.

Appendix G

Wycliffe Associates
P.O. Box 2000
Orange, CA 92867, USA
Phone: 714-639-9950
           800-THE-WORD
EM: wycliffe_associates@wycliffe.org
WEB SITE: www.wycliffeassociates.org

Wycliffe Associates is a ministry that supports the work of Wycliffe Bible Translators (WBT). More than 50,000 members and friends now serve WBT and experience the excitement and fulfillment of hands-on involvement in the task of Bible translation. Wycliffe Associates provides programs and services that allow people to become directly involved in Bible translation.

The history of Wycliffe Associates goes back to 1967 when a small group of businessmen became interested in helping WBT. These friends wanted to find ways to come alongside Wycliffe translators and support personnel by doing the things that would allow WBT to focus more fully on the work of Bible translation.

In addition to providing resources for Wycliffe, these visionary individuals wanted to provide ways that others (like themselves) could become involved in Bible translation.

The first challenge that faced this small group of businessmen was to find ways of serving Wycliffe and to pass those same opportunities of service on to their fellow Christians. But where would the financial resources come from?

How could they pay for printing a newsletter, mailing the receipts, and renting a building?

And so the idea of a "membership organization" was born. People interested in Wycliffe and willing to stand behind the translators would pay their own way. Through membership dues, Wycliffe Associates members would cover the necessary costs and build a solid base of support for

Wycliffe. Furthermore, volunteers working on a project would pay their own expenses. With these two parameters, Wycliffe Associates would be able to fulfill this dual role of supporting Wycliffe Bible Translators and providing involvement opportunities to interested Christians.

Wycliffe Associates currently offers the following involvement opportunities:

1. The Banquet Ministry: Twice a year in more than one hundred cities per tour, the Banquet Ministry provides information about world-wide progress in Bible translation. Guests have the opportunity to support the work of Bible translation by making a faith promise commitment. Banquets also play a key role in recruiting translators and support personnel for WBT.

2. Chapters: Chapter members join in fellowship and partnership with others in their own community who are committed to Bible transla-tion. Involvement in a Wycliffe Associates Chapter includes hearing first-hand reports from missionaries, assisting with project funding, coordinating banquets in their area, volunteering or recruiting volunteers for construction projects, forming prayer groups, as well as providing mis-sionaries with linens and hospitality homes to overnight in when traveling.

3. Construction: Through this ministry, Wycliffe Associates pro-vides facilities for WBT across the USA and around the world. Experienced construction superintendents, skilled volunteers, and hard workers help build and equip translation centers, houses, schools, and other vital facilities that enable Wycliffe translators to work effectively and efficiently.

4. HELPS (Harnessing Every Lay Person's Skills): This program pro-vides hands-on office opportunities for those interested in assisting at one of three U.S. offices—Wycliffe Associates in Orange, California; Wycliffe Bible Translators in Orlando, Florida; and SIL International at the International Linguistics Center in Dallas, Texas.

5. Hospitality Roster: Wycliffe Associates people who sign up for the Hospitality Roster open their homes to WBT members traveling in the USA. This unique ministry offers Wycliffe members a safe place to stay without using up their limited financial resources, and offers Wycliffe Associates families the opportunity to meet missionaries in person and hear behind-the-scenes stories of firsthand experiences.

6. Linen Closets: One of the favorite ministries of Wycliffe members and Wycliffe Associates friends and supporters is the Linen Closet

Ministry. This ministry provides a brand-new set of sheets and towels to each Wycliffe family member when they go out to their assignment or return for furlough. What seems a small gift blesses these families as they make significant transitions.

7. Prayer Ministry: Wycliffe Associates members and friends support Bible translation through their prayers, prayer groups, prayer journeys to the field, and by receiving the weekly prayer watch message—either by e-mail or by calling the 24-hour telephone prayer line.

8. Short-term Mission Trips: These trips provide volunteer opportunities for both groups and individuals to various WBT, SIL and Wycliffe Associates projects and offices throughout the USA and all around the world. Opportunities to serve include: prayer journeys, child care during branch conferences, construction and/or maintenance trips, and substitute teaching.

While Wycliffe Associates is an organization, the true heart of Wycliffe Associates lies in the tens of thousands of volunteers who have given their time, prayers, and resources and who have shared the vision of Bible Translation with their friends. As a result of their efforts Wycliffe Associates is privileged to be making a daily difference in the lives of Wycliffe missionaries and their far-reaching ministry.

Appendix H

Bible Translation and Literacy (BTL)
P.O. Box 44456, Nairobi, Kenya
Rev. Micah Amukobole, General Secretary
PHONE: 254 (2) 724-776
                    254 (2) 724-767
EM: GS_BTL@sil.org

In many countries around the world, Christians and churches indigenous to that country develop their own Bible translation organization. BTL is one of over a dozen National Bible Translation Organizations (NBTOs) with which SIL and WBT are involved. SIL and WBT provide these NBTOs with resources, consultants, and training to develop their own consultants. Working together, WBT and NBTOs know they can produce better translations. BTL was formed in 1981 and since that time has been headed up by Rev. Micah Amukobole. John C. Mpalampa served as chairman of the board of directors from 1981 to 1990. Major John Seii (retired) took over the mantle from Mr. Mpalampa and continues serving BTL in this way.

BTL works in twelve of the fifty-eight languages of Kenya. Since its inception, BTL has published and dedicated one New Testament. A second one will be dedicated in August 2000.

Cyrus Murage serves as full-time literacy coordinator for BTL. David Diida joined BTL in early 1991 after translating the complete Bible into Borana, his mother tongue, under the auspices of the Bible Society of Kenya. He now carries out literacy work among his Borana people.

By the year 2025, BTL, working together with other organizations, plans to see that translation of Scripture has begun in every language group in Kenya where there is a need.

Appendix I

Quest
P.O. Box 629200
Orlando, FL 32862-8200
PHONE: 800-388-1928
FAX: 407-852-3651
WEB SITE: www.wbt.org/quest

Quest, Wycliffe's new-member intake course, is described in a WBT brochure as "a three-week discovery experience...also a busy, often intense time of study, exploration and evaluation." (*Wycliffe's Quest. An inquiring step toward membership.*)

This three-week course is held around eight times a year at a mountaintop retreat center two miles from the resort town of Idyllwild, California. At Quest, young people, and some not-so-young people, are given an opportunity to "look over Wycliffe" while Wycliffe looks them over.

Therefore the singles, couples and families who attend are either "seekers" or applicants to Wycliffe. For seekers, Quest is a discovery time when people learn more about themselves, missions, and Wycliffe. Those asking, "Is missions part of God's will for me?" or "Would my skills complement the work of Bible translation and is Wycliffe where God would want me to serve?" are encouraged to apply to Quest under the "seeker" category. They are assured that it is normal to have questions if one is considering mission service.

For those who are fairly sure God is leading them to join Wycliffe, Quest is part of the "joining" process.

In classes the staff, most of whom are seasoned overseas workers, give the participants time to:

1. Grow spiritually with group studies, worship, and sharing together.
2. Explore their unique gifts and strengths that God might use in the task of Bible translation.

3. Expand their understanding of how they would fit in a ministry in other lands.

4. Discover God's place for them in fulfilling the Great Commission, possibly on the Wycliffe team.

Appendix J

Intercultural Communications Course (ICC)

All Wycliffe Members in Training attend an ICC. These courses are held twice yearly, both at the JAARS Center in North Carolina and at the International Linguistics Center in Dallas, Texas.

Most new members to WBT will be serving in a culture different from the one in which they grew up. They will need to relate appropriately to that new culture where they live and work. They will be asking, "How do I communicate? What are the cultural signals and cues? Just how do I relate and minister?"

ICC helps prepare them to cross these bridges when they arrive overseas.